雙雙中文教材（14）
Chinese Language and Culture Course

中國古代科學技術 *Ancient Chinese Science and Technology*

王雙雙 編著

張羅蘊 畫

北京大學出版社
PEKING UNIVERSITY PRESS

圖書在版編目（CIP）數據

中國古代科學技術：繁體版／（美）王雙雙編著.—北京：北京大學出版社，2009.1
（雙雙中文教材14）
ISBN 978-7-301-14412-1

Ⅰ.中… Ⅱ.王… Ⅲ.①漢語–對外漢語教學–教材 ②自然科學史–中國–古代 Ⅳ.H195.4

中國版本圖書館CIP數據核字（2008）第168380號

書　　　　名：	中國古代科學技術
著作責任者：	王雙雙 編著
英 文 翻 譯：	王亦兵　馬艷霞
封 面 圖 案：	王金泰
責 任 編 輯：	孫嫻
標 準 書 號：	ISBN 978-7-301-14412-1／H・2097
出 版 發 行：	北京大學出版社
地　　　　址：	北京市海淀區成府路205號　100871
網　　　　址：	http://www.pup.cn
電　　　　話：	郵購部 62752015　發行部 62750672　編輯部 62752028　出版部 62754962
電 子 信 箱：	zpup@pup.pku.edu.cn
印 刷 者：	北京大學印刷廠
經 銷 者：	新華書店
	889毫米×1194毫米　16開本　9.75印張　156千字
	2009年1月第1版　2009年1月第1次印刷
定　　　　價：	90.00元（含課本、練習册和CD-ROM一張）

未經許可，不得以任何方式複製或抄襲本書之部分或全部內容。
版權所有，侵權必究
舉報電話：010-62752024
電子信箱：fd@pup.pku.edu.cn

前 言

《雙雙中文教材》是一套專門爲海外青少年編寫的中文課本，是我在美國八年的中文教學實踐基礎上編寫成的。在介紹這套教材之前，請讀一首小詩：

> 一雙神奇的手，
> 推開一扇窗。
> 一條神奇的路，
> 通向燦爛的中華文化。
>
> 鮑凱文　鮑維江
> 1998年

鮑維江和鮑凱文姐弟倆是美國生美國長的孩子，也是我的學生。1998年冬，他們送給我的新年賀卡上的小詩，深深地打動了我的心。我把這首詩看成我文化教學的"回聲"。我要傳達給海外每位中文老師：我教給他們（學生）中國文化，他們思考了、接受了、回應了。這條路走通了！

語言是交際的工具，更是一種文化和一種生活方式，所以學習中文也就離不開中華文化的學習。漢字是一種古老的象形文字，她從遠古走來，帶有大量的文化信息，但學起來並不容易。使學生增強興趣、減小難度，走出苦學漢字的怪圈，走進領悟中華文化的花園，是我編寫這套教材的初衷。

學生不論大小，天生都有求知的慾望，都有欣賞文化美的追求。中華文化本身是魅力十足的。把這宏大而玄妙的文化，深入淺出地，有聲有色地介紹出來，讓這迷人的文化如涓涓細流，一點一滴地滲入學生們的心田，使學生們逐步體味中國文化，是我編寫這套教材的目的。

為此我將漢字的學習放入文化介紹的流程之中同步進行，讓同學們在學中國地理的同時，學習漢字；在學中國歷史的同時，學習漢字；在學中國哲學的同時，學習漢字；在學中國科普文選的同時，學習漢字……

這樣的一種中文學習，知識性強，趣味性強；老師易教，學生易學。當學生們合上書本時，他們的眼前是中國的大好河山，是中國五千年的歷史和妙不可言的哲學思維，是奔騰的現代中國……

總之，他們瞭解了中華文化，就會探索這片土地，熱愛這片土地，就會與中國結下情緣。

最後我要衷心地感謝所有熱情支持和幫助我編寫教材的老師、家長、學生、朋友和家人，特別是老同學唐玲教授、何茜老師、我姐姐王欣欣編審及我女兒Uta Guo年復一年的鼎力相助。可以說這套教材是大家努力的結果。

王雙雙

說　明

　　《雙雙中文教材》是一套專門為海外學生編寫的中文教材。它是由美國加州王雙雙老師和中國專家學者共同努力，在海外多年的實踐中編寫出來的。全書共20冊，識字量2500個，包括了從識字、拼音、句型、短文的學習，到初步的較系統的中國文化的學習。教材大體介紹了中國地理、歷史、哲學等方面的豐富內容，突出了中國文化的魅力。課本知識面廣，趣味性強，深入淺出，易教易學。

　　這套教材體系完整、構架靈活、使用面廣。學生可以從零起點開始，一直學完全部課程20冊，也可以將後11冊（10～20冊）的九個文化專題和第五冊（漢語拼音）單獨使用，這樣便於開設中國哲學、地理、歷史等專門課程以及假期班、短期中國文化班、拼音速成班的高中和大學使用，符合了美國AP中文課程的目標和基本要求。

　　本書是《雙雙中文教材》的第十四冊，適用於已學習掌握1000個以上漢字的學生使用。中華民族五千年歷史積澱的巨大創造力不僅表現在她獨特的文化上，也體現在她古代偉大的科學技術成就上。本書通過一個個生動的故事向學生們介紹了部分中國古代科學技術發現和發明的過程，如：指南針、造紙術、活字印刷術和火藥等四大發明，陶瓷製作和絲綢紡織技術的發明、發展，茶葉的種植及研究，以及中國古代在醫藥學、天文學、水利工程等方面取得的重大成果。通過學習，學生們不僅能學到一些科技知識，而且能從一個側面進一步瞭解中國古代的文化、地理和歷史，從而加深對中華文明的認識。

編者

課程設置

一年級	中文課本（第一冊）	中文課本（第二冊）	中文課本（第三冊）
二年級	中文課本（第四冊）	中文課本（第五冊）	中文課本（第六冊）
三年級	中文課本（第七冊）	中文課本（第八冊）	中文課本（第九冊）
四年級	中國成語故事		中國地理常識
五年級	中國古代故事		中國神話傳說
六年級	中國古代科學技術		中國文學欣賞
七年級	中國詩歌欣賞		中文科普閱讀
八年級	中國古代哲學		中國歷史（上）
九年級	中國歷史（下）		小說閱讀，中文SAT II
十年級	中文SAT II（強化班）		小說閱讀，中文SAT II 考試

目 錄

第 一 課　　四大發明（一）指南針 ……………………1

第 二 課　　四大發明（二）蔡倫造紙 …………………6

第 三 課　　四大發明（三）火藥 ………………………11

第 四 課　　四大發明（四）活字印刷術 ………………18

第 五 課　　張衡和他的地動儀 …………………………23

第 六 課　　絲綢和絲綢之路 ……………………………29

第 七 課　　茶神陸羽 ……………………………………36

第 八 課　　李春造橋 ……………………………………43

第 九 課　　"藥王"孫思邈 ………………………………49

第 十 課　　李時珍和他的《本草綱目》…………………56

第十一課　　都江堰 ………………………………………62

第十二課　　中國瓷器 ……………………………………71

生 字 表 ……………………………………………………79

生 詞 表 ……………………………………………………83

第一課

四大發明（一）
指南針

大約在2000多年前的戰國時期，中國人就發現磁石可以用來指方向。他們把天然磁石磨成一個光滑的小勺，放在又平又滑的"地盤"上，讓它自由轉動。勺子停下來的時候，勺把指的方向，總是南方，這就是最早的指南針，當時稱為"司南"。

王金泰 畫

1000多年前，中國人又發明了"指南魚"。指南魚是用2寸長、5分①寬的薄鐵片做成一條魚的形狀，魚肚部分凹下去一些，可以像小船一樣浮在水面上；然後進行人工磁化，就是把鐵片與天然磁石放在一起緊緊地挨著，時間久了，鐵片就有了磁性。這樣，只要有一碗水，把指南魚放在水面上，就可以指示南北方向了。

可是指南魚的磁性有時太弱，不太好用。後來人們把一根鋼針放在磁石上磨，使鋼針變成了磁針。磁針穿上幾根乾草，就可以浮在水面指示方向。還有一種方法是用一根細線把磁針掛在沒有風的地方，下面配有寫著方位的盤，磁針和盤一起組成了真正的指南針。這就是可以準確指示方向的羅盤。

到了12世紀（北宋），中國的海船上就裝有羅盤。這樣不管是白天還是黑夜，陰雨還是大霧，船都不會迷失方向，使海上航行安全多了。

13世紀初（南宋），中國的指南針傳到歐洲，大大促進了世界航海業的發展。

---

① 分——長度單位，10分等於1寸。

第一課

生詞

cí 磁	magnetic	fāngwèi 方位	direction and position
sháo 勺	spoon; ladle	luó pán 羅盤	compass
zì yóu 自由	freely; freedom	wù 霧	fog
báo 薄	thin; flimsy	mí shī 迷失	lose (one's way, etc.)
āo 凹	cave in; sunken	chū 初	in the early part of; at the beginning of
zhǐ shì 指示	direct; instruct	cù jìn 促進	promote; advance
gāng 鋼	steel	hánghǎi 航海	navigation
pèi 配	equip with		

聽寫

發明　鋼　小勺　自由　羅盤　霧　初　航海　方位

迷失　*促進　配

注：*號以後的字詞為選做題，後同。

比一比

{ 雨（下雨）
  霧（大霧）

{ 足（足球）
  促（促進）

{ 雪（白雪）
  雷（打雷）

3

中國古代科學技術

詞語運用

司南　司機　公司

中國最早的指南針叫司南。

李明的叔叔是開大卡車的司機。

蘋果電腦公司就在離我家不遠的地方。

航海　航空

你想當一名航海家嗎？

每年春節航空公司都很忙。

米飯　迷路

小文文就愛吃麵包、點心，不愛吃米飯。

如果你在野外旅行，千萬要帶上指南針，這樣才不會迷路。

反義詞

薄——厚　　　　　　天然——人工

判斷對錯

1. 戰國時期，中國人已經發明了指南針。　　　＿＿對＿＿錯
2. 12世紀中國人將指南針用於航海。　　　　　＿＿對＿＿錯
3. 陰雨大霧，有了指南針，船就不會迷失方向。＿＿對＿＿錯
4. 羅盤不可以指方向。　　　　　　　　　　　＿＿對＿＿錯

Lesson One

Four Great Inventions (I)
The Compass

During the Warring States Period some 2,000 years ago, natural magnetite was discovered in China as useful devices for identifying direction. The ancient Chinese shaped the natural magnetite into a small, glossy ladle and put it on a smooth, flat plate on the ground, and let it turn freely. When the ladle stopped moving, the handle would always point to the South. This was the first compass in the world and the ancient Chinese named it Sinan (meaning south-pointing ladle).

About 1,000 years later, the ancient Chinese invented the "Guide Fish". The "Guide Fish" was made of a thin piece of iron figure that looked like a fish. Its length was two cun (approximately 6.66 centimeters) and the width was five *fen* (approximately 1.65 centimeters). As it had an abdomen that curved inwards, the "Guide Fish" could float on water like a small boat. The "Guide Fish" was manually magnetized after being tied to natural magnetite for a while. This caused the iron piece to turn into a magnet and the "Guide Fish" could identify the North-South direction when placed on the surface of a bowl of water.

However, the magnetism in the "Guide Fish" was weak and not very effective. The ancient Chinese went on to try to grind a steel needle on a magnetite to transfer its magnetic properties over to the needle. A few straws of hay were then threaded into the needle and the needle could float on water and identify directions. Another method was to tie the magnetic needle to a rope in a place where there was no wind nor draft and let it dangle freely. A plate with directions (North, South, East, and West) written on it was placed below the needle. The magnetic needle, with the plate underneath, constituted the "real" compass. This device was able to identify directions accurately, and it became known as *Luopan* (meaning compass).

In the 12th century, during the Northern Song Dynasty, the compass was used for sea navigation. The people depended on it to keep them from getting lost day and night, especially on rainy and foggy days. Sea navigation became much safer because of this invention.

The compass from China was introduced to Europe at the beginning of the 13th century, during the Southern Song Dynasty. This contributed greatly to the development of worldwide navigation.

第二課

四大發明（二）
蔡倫造紙

中國古代，在沒有發明紙以前，人們大多把文字寫在竹簡上。

竹簡很笨重，不方便，有的官員寫一份報告給皇帝，要由兩個人吃力地抬進宮去。那時，還有人用帛寫字。帛是絲織品，很輕便，但是非常貴，要用720斤大米纔能換一匹帛，一般人根本用不起。

西漢時已有人開始用絲絮和麻造紙，但這種麻紙很粗糙。東漢時有個叫蔡倫的人，想要造出一種更好的紙，給人們寫字。他看到人們把蠶繭煮熟後放在席子上，再放到河裏，用棍子敲打成爛絲綿，再把絲綿揭下來，席子上留下一層薄薄的絮片。絮片曬乾揭下來就能在上面寫字了。雖然絲絮片無法大量生產，但是這個方法讓蔡倫想到樹皮、麻頭、舊漁網和破布等可以做原料。他做了很多試驗，把樹皮、麻頭、舊漁網和破布一起煮成漿，再放在席子上，刮成薄薄一層，放在太陽底下曬乾。這就是那時候世界上最好的紙。在這種紙上寫字又吃墨又光滑，十分理想。

公元105年，蔡倫把這一重大發明報告給皇帝。因為這樣造出的紙又輕又便宜又好用，人們都很喜歡，所以全國的人很快就都用上了紙。

造紙術在幾百年後傳到了朝鮮、日本、印度、阿拉伯和歐洲，促進了世界文化的發展。

王金泰 畫

生詞

cài lún	蔡倫	Cai Lun (*a name*)	jiē	揭	tear off
zhú jiǎn	竹簡	bamboo strips	shēng chǎn	生產	produce
bèn zhòng	笨重	cumbersome	jiù	舊	old; worn-out
bào gào	報告	report	yú wǎng	漁網	fishing net
bó	帛	silk	pò bù	破布	rag
guì	貴	expensive	yuán liào	原料	raw material
sī xù	絲絮	silk wadding	shì yàn	試驗	test; experiment
cū cāo	粗糙	coarse	jiāng	漿	pulp
cán jiǎn	蠶繭	silkworm cocoon	mò	墨	Chinese ink
gùn zi	棍子	stick	pián yi	便宜	cheap; affordable
sī mián	絲綿	silk floss	ā lā bó	阿拉伯	Arabia

聽寫

竹簡　棍子　粗糙　生產　試驗　破布　舊　墨

便宜　笨重　阿拉伯　*蔡

比一比

佈（分佈）
布（棉布）

料 ｛ 原料 / 布料 ｝

反義詞

破爛──完好　　　　　便宜──昂貴

新──舊　　　　　　　粗糙──精細

詞語運用

便宜　輕便　方便

這雙球鞋很便宜。

紙比竹簡輕便多了。

有了電視，看節目就方便多了。

簡單　竹簡

這道算術題很簡單。

古代人們把文字寫在竹簡上。

新　舊

昨天我買了一本新書。

我捨不得扔掉這件舊衣服。

判斷對錯

1. 古代沒有紙，人們常常把字寫在竹簡上。　　＿＿對＿＿錯

2. 蔡倫造出了又好用又方便的紙。　　＿＿對＿＿錯

3. 蔡倫造的紙不便宜。　　＿＿對＿＿錯

Lesson Two

Four Great Inventions (II)
The Paper Improved by Cai Lun

Before paper was invented, most ancient Chinese used to carve words on bamboo strips.

However, the bamboo strips were heavy and cumbersome, and this made it inconvenient to use. A report written on bamboo strips by an official would require two strong men to carry to the palace to be presented to the emperor. Besides bamboo strips, the richer Chinese wrote on silk as well, which was much lighter and portable. But this form of writing material was too expensive for the ordinary people. The cost of one pi (approximately 13 meters) of silk was equivalent to 360 kilograms of rice.

During the Western Han Dynasty, people used silk wadding and hemp to produce paper. But this type of paper was very coarse. It was only later during the Eastern Han Dynasty that Cai Lun made further contribution to the development of paper. Cai Lun wanted to make a better quality paper which would be affordable for ordinary folks. He noticed that some people boiled silkworm cocoons and spread them on mats. They then put the mats into the river before hitting them using sticks. This caused the cocoons to disintegrate into silk floss. The silk floss would then be torn off from the mat and there will be a thin, flaky layer of silk left on the mat. After the silk has dried up, the people will peel it off and use it as a form of writing material.

Although silk flakes could not be produced in large quantity, this method inspired Cai to use tree bark, bits of ropes, worn-out fishing nets and rags as raw materials for producing paper. He did numerous experiments: boiling various materials into pulp, spreading them onto mats, scraping them into a thin layer, and drying the layer under the sun. After many experiments, working by trial and error, he managed to produce the best and ideal paper in the world at that time for it had a smooth surface and absorbed ink well.

In A.D. 105, Cai reported his great invention to the Han emperor. As the paper was light, inexpensive and good in quality, it was readily accepted by people throughout China.

A few centuries later, this papermaking technique was introduced to the Korean Peninsula, Japan, India, Arabia and Europe and it revolutionized cultural development around the world.

第三課

四大發明（三）
火藥

春節是中國人最重要的節日。每到春節的夜晚，不管是城市還是農村，到處都可以看到快樂的孩子在放煙花和爆竹。在美麗的煙花和喜慶的爆竹聲中，人們迎來了新的一年。

煙花和爆竹是用什麼做成的呢？是用火藥做的。中國是世界上最早發明火藥的國家。

早在3000年前（商朝），中國人就會煉青銅。後來，2500多

王金泰 畫

年前（春秋時期）又學會煉鐵。這使許多煉丹術士夢想煉出長生不老的仙丹。他們不斷地在煉丹爐中試驗，有時煉丹爐會突然發出爆炸聲和冒出大火，把房頂燒掉。到公元1世紀（西漢），經過一次次的爆炸起火，人們終於發現把三樣東西：硫磺、硝石、木炭按照一定的比例混合在一起加熱，在高熱的情況下會發生爆炸，這就是火藥。火藥發明的時間大約在1500年前（唐朝）。

自從有了火藥，人類得到了一種前所未有的巨大力量。很快火藥就被用在武器上。唐朝末年，中國人發明了火藥箭，弓箭用上了火藥，增強了殺傷力。在宋朝，首都開封有一個很大的兵工場，火藥武器也越來越多地用於戰爭。宋朝與西夏作戰時，一次就用了25萬支火藥箭。另外，還有一種武器叫火球，點著後升入空中，爆炸時好像天上打雷，同時還飛出大量的石灰迷住敵人的眼睛。當時還發明了"突火槍"，就是把火藥裝在竹筒裏，然後放上像子彈一樣

的石子和小鐵塊。這是世界上最早的"槍"。同時火藥還被用來開山採礦和做成各種美麗的煙花和爆竹，供人們過年過節時使用。

公元1225年—1284年，火藥傳入印度，以後又傳入阿拉伯和歐洲。英、法等國家直到14世紀中期才使用火藥武器。

生詞

huǒ yào 火藥	gunpowder	bǐ lì 比例	proportion
yān huā 煙花	fireworks	hùn hé 混合	mix
bào zhú 爆竹	firecrackers	qián suǒ wèi yǒu 前所未有	unprecedented
liàn 煉	smelt; refine	lì liang 力量	strength; power
qīng tóng 青銅	bronze	wǔ qì 武器	weapon
lú 爐	stove; furnace	mò 末	end; last
bào zhà 爆炸	explode; explosion	qiāng 槍	gun
mù tàn 木炭	charcoal	zǐ dàn 子彈	bullet; pellet
àn zhào 按照	according to	gōng 供	provide; supply

聽寫

火藥　煙花　爐　子彈　槍　力量　末　混合　按照

武器　煉　青銅　*供　爆炸

比一比

量 { 力量
　　商量

混（混合）
棍（木棍）

炸（爆炸）
昨（昨天）
作（作業）

詞語運用

採礦　採花　彩虹

火藥可以用來開山採礦。

小白兔在山坡上採花。

下完雨後，天上出現了一道彩虹。

例子　比例

請你舉一個例子說明這個問題。

這個學校男生和女生人數的比例是 2：1。

按　按照

小明回到家門口，按了按門鈴，哥哥把門打開了。

我每次都按照老師的要求把課文大聲讀三遍。

判斷對錯

1. 春節的夜晚，孩子們喜歡放煙花和爆竹。　　　＿＿對＿＿錯

2. 煙花和爆竹是用火藥做的。　　　　　　　　　＿＿對＿＿錯

3. 唐朝末年火藥被用在軍事上。　　　　　　　　＿＿對＿＿錯

閱讀

勇敢的萬戶

　　自古以來，人們就夢想著像鳥兒一樣能飛，飛上高高的天空。聰明、勇敢的人們一次又一次地用各種辦法嘗試飛天。14世紀末，明朝就有一個被稱為"萬戶"的人，做了一次大膽的試驗。他在一把椅子後面裝上了47個大火箭，自己坐在椅子上，兩手各拿著一個大風箏，再讓人們把火箭點著，想靠火箭的推力和風箏上升的力量飛上天空。在一陣爆炸聲之後，他摔了下來。雖然試驗沒有成功，但是他的確很了不起。可以說萬戶是第一個"坐"火箭飛行的人。

Lesson Three
Four Great Inventions (III)
Gunpowder

Chinese New Year is the most important Chinese festival celebrated by all the Chinese. During Chinese New Year, children from both cities and the countryside can be seen happily lighting fireworks and crackers as they welcome the new year with the sounds of the beautiful fireworks and crackers.

But what are these fireworks and crackers made of? The answer is gunpowder. China was the first country to invent gunpowder.

As early as 3,000 years ago during the Shang Dynasty, the Chinese had already mastered the technology of smelting bronze. About 2,500 years ago during the Spring and Autumn Period, the Chinese had learnt to smelt iron as well. This inspired numerous "wizards" to dream of smelting and refining a mixture that could become an elixir of youth. They tirelessly conducted many experiments over their refining stoves. At times the stoves would suddenly ignite and explode through their roofs. It was the first century after A.D. 1, during the Western Han Dynasty, after many rounds of explosions, when the ancient Chinese discovered the recipe for gunpowder. They learnt that a huge explosion producing gunpowder was the result of mixing the right proportions of sulfur, niter, and charcoal together, heated to a suitably high temperature. Gunpowder was invented about 1,500 years ago during the Tang Dynasty.

Ever since its invention, the explosive had brought great unprecedented power to human beings and it did not take long for people to use it as a weapon. Towards the end of the Tang Dynasty, the Chinese invented gunpowder arrows and this greatly enhanced the potency of the traditional bow and arrow. During the Song Dynasty, a big arsenal, was located in the capital city Kaifeng, and more and more weapons that were developed from the explosive were adopted for warfare. During a battle between the Song Dynasty and the Western Xia Dynasty, each firing could use up 250,000 gunpowder arrows. Besides arrows, fireballs were also created and used for warfare purposes. The fireball was a cannon ball which would be lit up by gunpowder and it will catapult up to the sky towards the enemy's line. It would explode with a sound as loud as thunder, emitting lime powder at the same time which brings tears to the enemies' eyes. During that time, the *Tu-huo Qiang* (meaning "fire-spouting gun") was also invented. The army first filled gunpowder into bamboo tubes and then filled the tubes with pellets made up of pebbles and little iron bits. That was the first and earliest "gun" ever made. At the same time, gunpowder was also widely used in excavating mountains for mining purpose; as well as in creating beautiful fireworks and fire crackers during Chinese New Year celebrations.

Gunpowder was introduced to India between A.D. 1225 and A.D. 1284, before it was brought into Arabia and Europe. It was not until the mid 14th century that the British and French first used gunpowder as weapons.

Brave Wan Hu

Ever since ancient times, people have always been dreaming of being able to fly up to the sky like the birds. Many intelligent and brave people have tried over and over again to find a method or a means to fly. At the end of the 14th century, during the Ming Dynasty, a person called Wan Hu did an adventurous and dangerous experiment. He designed a chair by attaching 47 arrows coated with gunpowder behind. He sat on the chair, holding one big kite in each hand, and had someone detonate the arrows by bringing a flame to them. He had hoped to propel up into the sky through the force set off by the detonation which may be assisted by the kites. Unfortunately, although an explosive sound was heard and the arrows took off, Wan Hu fell to the ground. Even though he failed in the experiment, Wan Hu's idea was considered brilliant. We can also consider Wan Hu to be the first person to have taken a flight on the rocket. This is because the Chinese term for "rocket" is made up of the two characters— "fire" (火) and "arrow" (箭) — exactly the two elements that made up Wan Hu's "engine".

第四課

四大發明（四）
活字印刷術

中國古代在印刷術發明以前，書要一個字一個字地用手抄寫，速度很慢。

唐朝中期，人們發明了雕版印刷術，就是用刀按照書寫的字，一筆一筆地刻在一塊硬木上，再印刷。雕版印刷比起用手抄寫，不知快了多少。但是每塊雕版上的字都是固定在一起的，每換一次內容，就得重刻一次版，很不方便。

王金泰 畫

12世紀（北宋），有個叫畢昇的人發明了活字印刷術。

畢昇小時候，因為家窮，只讀了幾年書，就到一家印書的作坊去當工匠。畢昇的工作非常辛苦，一天到晚要整版整版地刻字。一次，他和朋友下棋，下著下著，他看看棋盤又看看棋子，突然想："如果印刷版上的字像棋子一樣，變成活的，那多好啊！"

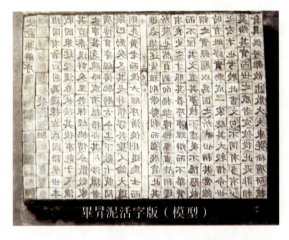
畢昇泥活字版（模型）

於是他開始一次次地試驗。他先在薄薄的膠泥上刻字，做成一個一個的字印，再用火燒硬，這就成了一個個像棋子一樣的"活"字。印書的時候，只要把"活"字按照稿件排在字盤上，用蠟固定住，壓平，便可以印刷了。印完以後，把"活"字拆下來，可以再次使用。這樣印書，又快又省力，還省錢。後來，元代的王幀(zhēn)又把畢昇的泥活字改為木活字。王幀還發明了轉盤活字法，這樣印書就更方便了。

活字印刷術是一個重大的發明，從此印書變得又快又簡單。後來印刷術傳到朝鮮、日本、阿拉伯和歐洲。

中國古代科學技術

生詞

yìn shuā 印刷	printing		xià qí 下棋	play chess
chāo xiě 抄寫	copy(by hand); transcribe		jiāo ní 膠泥	sticky clay
sù dù 速度	speed		gǎo jiàn 稿件	manuscript
diāo bǎn 雕版	block printing; engraving		là 蠟	wax
bì 畢	Bi (*a surname*)		yā 壓	press
zuō fang 作坊	workshop		chāi xia 拆下	take apart
gōng jàng 工匠	craftsman; artisan			

聽寫

印刷　抄寫　速度　工匠　稿件　壓　拆下

下棋　*作坊　蠟

比一比

少（多少）　　次（一次）　　其（其實）
抄（抄寫）　　砍（砍柴）　　期（日期）

反（相反）　　拆（拆下）　　棋（下棋）
版（出版）　　折（折斷）　　旗（彩旗）

詞語運用

出版　木板

這本書是什麼時候出版的？

舊金山的許多房子是用木板建造的。

下棋　星期　其實

杜丹下棋下得很好。

每星期四學校都有羽毛球比賽。

有人覺得學習好最重要，其實呢，身體好更重要。

學校　交給　膠泥

學校馬上就要放春假了。

我把禮物親手交給了哥哥。

膠泥是做"活"字的原料。

判斷對錯

1. 印刷術發明以前，書要一個字一個字地用手抄寫。　　___對___錯
2. 雕版印刷比用手抄寫快，但還是不方便。　　___對___錯
3. 北宋時期畢昇發明了活字印刷術。　　___對___錯

Lesson Four

Four Great Inventions (IV)
The Movable Type-Printing Press

Before the invention of the printing press, the ancient Chinese copied books character for character by hand, and this process took them a long time to finish copying a book.

In the middle of the Tang Dynasty, the ancient Chinese invented the block printing technique by carving all the characters found in a book onto a piece of hardwood block before printing it. Compared to copying by hand, this method was much more efficient. However, as the arrangement of the characters on each block was fixed, it required a new block for a new page and this involved a lot of work as well.

In the 12th century during the North Song Dynasty, a person named Bi Sheng invented the portable type printing technique.

Due to poverty, Bi Sheng only had a few years of school education before he started working in a printing workshop. He worked very hard and carved one block after another around the clock. One day, while he was playing Chinese chess with a friend, he could not help but stared back and forth between the chess board and the pieces. A thought occurred to him: "What if all the characters on the printing block are movable like the chess pieces?"

He began to put the idea into experiments. Firstly, he carved individual characters on squares of sticky clay and baked them to make clay pieces like the chess pieces. He then composed the text by arranging the characters in a frame, secured them with wax, and pressed them to produce a flat surface before printing. After printing, the characters could be taken out of the frame and stored for future use. This method was efficient, as it saved both energy and money. Later on, instead of using clay, Wang Zhen of the Yuan Dynasty used wooden type and stored movable characters on revolving trays to improve work efficiency.

The movable type printing technique was a significant invention which made printing more efficient and convenient. This method was subsequently introduced to the Korean Peninsula, Japan, Arabia and Europe.

第五課

張衡和他的地動儀

晚上，滿天的星星像無數珍珠掛在天空。一個孩子坐在院子裏，仰著頭，指著天空數星星。一顆，兩顆……一直數到了幾百顆。奶奶笑著說："傻孩子，又在數星星了。那麼多星星，一閃一閃地亂動，眼都花了。你能數得清嗎？"孩子說："奶奶，能看得見，就能數得清。星星是動，可不是亂動。您看，這顆星和那顆星，它們離得總是一樣遠。"

張衡（公元78年—139年）

爺爺走過來說："孩子，你看得很仔細。天上的星星是在動，可是，它們之間的距離是不變的。我們的祖先把它們分成一組一組的，還給它們起了名字。"爺爺停了停，指著北邊的天空，說："你們看，那七顆星，連起來像一把勺子，叫北斗星。離它們不遠的那顆星，叫北極星。北斗星總是繞著北極星轉。"

爺爺說的話是真的嗎？這孩子一夜沒睡好，幾次起來看星星。他想知道，北斗星是不是像爺爺說的那樣繞著北極星慢慢轉動。

這個數星星的孩子叫張衡（公元78年—139年），是漢朝人。他長大以後發明了測定地震方位的地動儀和演示日月星辰運行的渾天儀，成為一位偉大的天文學家。

張衡的地動儀，造於公元132年，是世界上最早的地震儀器。地動儀是用銅製造的，上面有八條龍，分別朝著八個方向。每條龍的嘴裏含著一個小銅球。哪個方向發生地震，那個方向的龍就吐出銅球，落在下面的青蛙嘴裏。

公元138年的一天，突然地動儀朝西的龍吐出銅球，落入青蛙嘴裏。過了幾天，洛陽西邊一千里遠的隴西派人送來消息，那裏發生了地震。地動儀測出的地震方向和時間都是對的。

地動儀（模型）

第五課

生詞

zhāng héng 張衡	Zhang Heng (a scientist and writer of the East Han Dynasty)	dì zhèn 地震	earthquake
zhēn zhū 珍珠	pearl	yǎn shì 演示	demonstrate
yǎng 仰	face upward; look up	hún tiān yí 渾天儀	Armillary Sphere (*a model of the celestial sphere*)
jù lí 距離	distance	tiān wén xué 天文學	astronomy
zǔ xiān 祖先	ancestors	zhì zào 製造	produce
běi dǒu xīng 北斗星	Big Dipper	luò yáng 洛陽	Luoyang(the capital city of the East Han)
cè dìng 測定	determine (through measuring or testing)	lǒng xī 隴西	Western Gansu

聽寫

仰　珍珠　距離　祖先　地震　演示　製造

測定　北斗星　天文學

比一比

祖（祖先）／組（小組）　　演｛演示／表演｝　　離｛距離／離開｝　　珍｛珍珠／珍稀｝

25

詞語運用

數學　數一數

張春明非常喜歡數學。

熊媽媽說："小黑熊，快把地裏的玉米數一數！"

亂動　颳風

上課時要坐好，不要亂動。

北京的春天常常颳大風。

兒子　仔細

爸爸讓兒子幫助媽媽幹活。

讀書要仔細，不要馬虎。

判斷對錯

1. 張衡小時候能數幾百顆星星。　　　　　　　___對___錯
2. 天上的星星在不停地亂動。　　　　　　　　___對___錯
3. 爺爺指著南邊的天空說："那七顆星，連起來像一把勺子，叫北斗星。"　　　　　　　___對___錯
4. 張衡聽完爺爺的話就睡覺了。　　　　　　　___對___錯
5. 張衡是漢朝偉大的天文學家。　　　　　　　___對___錯

6. 張衡製造了渾天儀並且發明了地動儀。　　＿＿對＿＿錯

7. 張衡的地動儀不是世界上最早的地震儀。　　＿＿對＿＿錯

小知識

祖沖之

中國古代有一位著名的科學家叫祖沖之（公元429年—500年）。他計算出圓周率（π）在3.1415926到3.1415927之間，第一次把圓周率推算到小數點後七位。一千年以後，阿拉伯數學家纔算出比祖沖之的計算更精確的圓周率。

祖沖之
（公元429年—500年）

Lesson Five

Zhang Heng and His Seismoscope

One night, a boy was sitting in the courtyard, looking up and pointing at the numerous pearly stars in the sky, counting them. "One, two...," he counted several hundred of them. His grandmother laughed, and asked him, "Silly boy, there you go again. There are so many stars twinkling in the sky and your eyes must be tired from looking at them. How can you possibly count them all?" The boy answered, "But Granny, surely we can keep a count on what we can see. Although the stars move around, they move in regular patterns too." "Look," he added, "The distance between this star and that one is always the same."

Grandpa came over and said to him, "You're right, son. The stars in the sky move, but the distance between them is always the same. Our ancestors grouped them in clusters and they even named each cluster of stars." Grandpa pointed to the north and said: "Look, there are seven stars over there; if you connect them in a line, you will find that the pattern resembles a ladle and this is why its name is 'Big Dipper'." He added, "The bright one close to them is the North Star, and the Big Dipper always rotates around it."

Did Grandpa mean what he said? The boy could not sleep that night as he kept getting up to check the position of the two star clusters. He wanted to know whether his grandfather was right and whether the Dipper rotated around the North Star slowly.

The boy counting the stars was Zhang Heng (A.D. 78 -A.D.139) of the Han Dynasty. He grew up and became a great astronomer. He invented the seismoscope, a device designed to measure the position of earthquakes. He also invented the Armillary Sphere which showed the movement of the sun, the moon, and the stars.

The seismoscope invented by Zhang Heng in A.D. 132 was the first seismic instrument to be invented in the world. It was made of copper, and on it were eight dragons pointing at eight different directions respectively. Each dragon had a small copper ball in its mouth. If an earthquake had occurred, the dragon pointing at the epicenter would spit the copper ball into the mouth of the frog under it.

One day in A.D. 138, the ball in the mouth of the dragon facing the west suddenly fell out into the mouth of the waiting frog. Several days later, official reports came from Western Gansu to report that there had been an earthquake there. Western Gansu was 500km west to the capital city of Luoyang. It was proven that both the direction and the time measured by Zhang Heng's seismoscope were extremely precise.

第六課

絲綢和絲綢之路

一、絲綢

　　中國自古以來就盛產絲綢，被稱為"絲綢之國"。早在五六千年以前，中國人就養蠶，用蠶絲織成絲綢做衣服穿。絲綢的衣服又柔軟美麗又涼快。到了漢代，中國的絲綢紡織技術已相當發達。1972年，在湖南長沙馬王堆漢墓中發現的精美絲織品就是證明。唐宋時期，絲織品已經是各式各樣，美麗非凡。唐代織造的一種絲綢非常薄，兩面都有花紋，掛在窗戶上還能透過光線。另外，還有一種用百鳥的羽毛和蠶絲織成的裙子，正看是一色，側看是一色；白天看是一色，燈下看又是一色，十分神奇。

　　據說，古羅馬的凱(kǎi)撒(sā)大帝有一次穿著一件中國絲袍到劇場看戲，絲袍華麗無比，光彩奪目，引起了全場的轟動。

中國古代科學技術

二、絲綢之路

漢朝初年,匈奴(xiōng nú)常常進犯漢朝國土,漢朝皇帝(武帝)於公元前139年派張騫(qiān)出使西域(中亞、西亞),為的是聯合西域各國共同打匈奴。張騫走到半路就被匈奴抓住了,讓他去放羊。十年後,他逃了出來,繼續往西走,經過草原、沙漠終於到了西域的大宛(yuān)國。大宛國的國王聽說他是漢朝的使節,對他很熱情,請他吃酒席。席上有大蒜、胡蘿蔔和葡萄酒等好多東西他都從來沒有見過。後來他詳細地把西域各國的山川、地理位置、經濟情況、物產、人口、兵力、風俗等寫成了文字,報告給皇帝。

公元前123年,漢朝皇帝出兵打敗了匈奴。從此,漢朝去西域的道路就開通了。漢朝皇帝又派張騫帶著許多禮物第二次去西域各國訪問,受到熱情接待。西域各國也派使節到長安訪問。從

那以後，西域各族和漢族的交流多了起來。漢族人種起了西域的葡萄、胡蘿蔔。西域各族從漢族得到了絲綢和鐵器，並向漢族學習了製造鐵器和鑿井的技術。

漢朝還修建了道路，並派軍隊保護商隊的安全。從此中國的絲綢源源不斷地由長安運到西亞和歐洲。這就是有名的"絲綢之路"。

生詞

fǎng zhī 紡織	spinning and weaving	jì xù 繼續	continue
mù 墓	tomb	rè qíng 熱情	enthusiastic; warm
gè shì gè yàng 各式各樣	of various kinds or styles; all kinds of	jiǔ xí 酒席	banquet; feast
		dà suàn 大蒜	garlic
huā wén 花紋	decorative pattern	hú luó bo 胡蘿蔔	carrot
qún zi 裙子	skirt	pú táo 葡萄	grape
cè 側	side	xiáng xì 詳細	in detail
sī páo 絲袍	silk robe	wèi zhì 位置	location
guāng cǎi duó mù 光彩奪目	dazzlingly bright; brilliant	fēng sú 風俗	social custom
hōng dòng 轟動	create a stir; cause a sensation	jiē dài 接待	receive; reception
jìn fàn 進犯	intrude into; invade	jiāo liú 交流	exchange

中國古代科學技術

聽寫

紡織　裙子　側　胡蘿蔔　詳細　大蒜　葡萄　酒席

各式各樣　熱情　*花紋　風俗

比一比

俗 { 風俗　俗話　通俗 }　　席 { 主席　酒席 }　　{ 文（文字）　紋（花紋）　蚊（蚊子） }

詞語運用

技術　算術

西域各族從漢族人那裏學會了鑿井的技術。

小蘭蘭喜歡上算術課。

羊群　裙子

天黑了，爸爸趕著羊群回家了。

商店裏有很多美麗的絲綢裙子。

考試　　各式各樣

明天上午姐姐有中文考試。

晚會上，同學們穿著各式各樣美麗的衣服來跳舞。

源源不斷

開通了絲綢之路，中國的絲綢源源不斷地運到西亞和歐洲。

判斷對錯

1. 中國生產絲綢有五六千年的歷史了。　　　＿＿對＿＿錯

2. 絲綢的衣服又柔軟又暖和。　　　　　　　＿＿對＿＿錯

3. 唐代有人用百鳥的羽毛織裙子。　　　　　＿＿對＿＿錯

4. 張騫出使西域是漢朝的事情。　　　　　　＿＿對＿＿錯

5. 大蒜、胡蘿蔔和葡萄酒等東西是從西域傳入中國的。　　　　　　　　　　　　　　　＿＿對＿＿錯

6. 西域各族向漢族學習了造鐵器和鑿井的技術。　　　　　　　　　　　　　　　　　　＿＿對＿＿錯

7. 大約從公元前1世紀開始，中國的絲綢就通過"絲綢之路"運到了西亞和歐洲。　　＿＿對＿＿錯

Lesson Six

Silk and the Silk Road
Silk

China has always been famous for its silk production even in its ancient years and this led to the country being named "The Nation of Silk." In fact, as long as five or six thousand years ago, the ancient Chinese raised silkworm, wove silk fabric, and made them into clothes, that were soft, beautiful, and pleasantly cool. During the Han Dynasty, the silk industry reached a relative high. This fact was proven when a large amount of exquisite silk products were excavated from the Han Tomb at Mawangdui in Changsha, Hunan Province in 1972. A wide variety of beautiful Chinese silk products were already available as early as the Tang and Song Dynasty. A form of translucent silk fabric known for the decorative motifs on both sides of the fabric was first woven during the Tang Dynasty and its translucent texture allowed light to penetrate when hung on windows. Another famous Chinese silk product was a silk skirt that was woven with the feathers of 100 different species of birds. What made the skirt so fascinating was that it always had a different tint when admired from under various light sources and directions.

It is said that Caesar, the Great Roman Emperor, once went to the theatre in a robe made of Chinese silk. The silk robe was so magnificent and brilliant that it attracted the attention of the entire audience in the theatre.

The Silk Road

In the early Han Dynasty, the Hsiung-Nu (a nomadic people from Central Asia) often invaded the land of the Han Dynasty. During the reign of Emperor Wu (Wu Di) of the Han Dynasty, in A.D. 139, the emperor sent his envoy, Zhang Qian, on a diplomatic mission to the Western Regions covering present Central Asia and Western Asia for the first time to seek the cooperation of the countries from (the) Western Regions to unite and fight against the Hsiung-Nu. Zhang Qian was captured by the Hsiung-Nu while he was on his way. He was then forced to work as a shepherd for a noble Hsiung-Nu man. Ten years later, he managed to escape, and, remembering his diplomatic mission, Zhang Qian continued journeying towards the west. He traveled through grassland and desserts and finally reached the kingdom of Dawan. Recognizing that he was an envoy sent by the Han Emperor, the Dawan king gave him a warm welcome and invited him to a banquet. It was during one of these banquets that Zhang first saw garlic, carrot and wine. He decided to conduct a thorough investigation and research on the areas around the mountains and the rivers. Besides these Zhang Xian also studied the geographical location, the local products, population and armed forces, and local customs of all the countries in the region; before reporting his findings to the Emperor of Han Dynasty.

In 123 B.C., the Emperor of Han Dynasty finally defeated the Hsiung-Nu and since then, the highway between the area under the Han Dynasty, and the Western Regions had been opened for all travel-

ers. Zhang Qian had a second chance to visit the Western Regions again. This time, he brought many presents along with him and had warm receptions from the kings of the western countries. These kings also sent envoys to Chang'an, the capital city at that time. This was the beginning of a long history of economic and cultural exchanges between the Western Regions and the Han people. The Han people learned to grow plants commonly found in the Western Regions, such as grape and carrot; while the western nations received silk and iron utensils; as well as techniques of making iron tools and digging wells; from the Han tribal group.

During the Han Dynasty, the government constructed roads and also sent armies to protect traveling businessmen. Ever since then, silk products have traveled a long way starting from Chang'an to Western Asia and Europe. This route has been famously named the Silk Road.

第七課

茶神陸羽

唐代有位著名的茶葉專家叫陸羽。

陸羽小時是個孤兒，從小在寺院裏長大。他小時候上山砍柴，手常被劃破，雙腿也被蟲子叮咬而紅腫生瘡。還好山上有位砍柴的老人，常為他用茶水清洗傷口，然後把茶葉搗爛敷在上面，傷口很快就好了。

有一次，陸羽上山砍柴，採了些野果吃，不料吃了以後上吐下瀉，又是砍柴的老人讓他喝了茶葉和芥(jiè)菜花煮的湯才好起來。從這以後，陸羽覺得茶葉很神奇，想寫一本介紹茶葉的書，讓天下人都瞭解茶葉，喜歡茶葉，用茶葉來幫助人們強身健體。

於是他動手從古書中查找有關茶的資料，但是發現資料很少。他又親自到產茶的地區去瞭解茶葉的特性、種植和加工方法。公元760年，陸羽帶著全部資料來到湖州，住在一座破廟中，開始了他的寫書生活。四年過去了，他終於寫完了中國歷史上第一部全面介紹茶的書《茶經》。

《茶經》問世以後，人們互相傳抄。茶經的流傳大大地促進了茶葉的生產和發展。從此人們稱《茶經》的作者陸羽為"茶神"。

王金泰 畫

生詞

zhuān jiā 專家	expert		chá zhǎo 查找	look for
gū ér 孤兒	orphan		zī liào 資料	material
sì yuàn 寺院	temple		liǎo jiě 瞭解	understand
huá pò 劃破	scratched		tè xìng 特性	specific property or characteristics
dǎo làn 搗爛	pound sth. into pulp; mash			
fū 敷	apply (powder, etc.)		zhòng zhí 種植	plant; cultivate
shàng tù xià xiè 上吐下瀉	suffer from vomiting and diarrhea		jiā gōng 加工	process
tāng 湯	soup		zuò zhě 作者	author
jiè shào 介紹	introduce			

聽寫

專家　上吐下瀉　介紹　資料　瞭解　加工　查找

種植　湯　作者　*特性　孤兒

比一比

解 { 解開 / 瞭解　　　孤 { 孤獨 / 孤兒　　　瀉 { 上吐下瀉 / 瀉藥

料 { 不料 / 材料 }   寫 { 寫字 / 寫詩 }

多音字

huá 劃
huá 劃破

huà 劃
huà 區劃

詞語運用

孤兒　狐狸

陸羽小時候是個孤兒。

狐狸常常偷雞吃。

判斷對錯

1. 喝茶可以強健身體。　　　　　　　　　　___對___錯

2. 老人為陸羽用茶水清洗傷口，傷口很快就好了。　　　　　　　　　　　　　　　　　　___對___錯

3. 《茶經》是漢朝的陸羽寫的。　　　　　___對___錯

4. 《茶經》是中國歷史上第一部全面介紹茶的書。

　　　　　　　　　　　　　　　　　　___對___錯

5. 茶葉是中國的特產。　　　　　　　　　　___對___錯

閱讀

茶文化

茶在中國有三千年歷史了。7世紀（隋suí唐）時，茶成為家家戶戶一日不可缺少的飲料。後來城市裏出現了茶館。朋友們在茶館裏一邊喝茶，一邊談話；或者一邊喝茶，一邊看節目、聽故事。茶館是放鬆精神和朋友聚jù會的好地方。客人來了倒上一杯茶，是中國人的禮儀和習俗。

茶是一種健康的飲料。茶性溫和，可以提神、助消化、利尿niào。中國人常靠喝茶健身。人們也常舉行茶會，或在宴yàn會上以茶代酒，以健康的方式聯誼yì。

茶文化還表現在中國人的哲zhé學思想中。有人說中國人的性格像茶，總是清醒、理智地看世界。在社會生活中主張和諧xié，互相幫助。平和、理性是茶文化的特點。

陶製茶具（謝光輝　攝）

Lesson Seven

Lu Yu, the God of the Tea

During the Tang Dynasty, there was an expert, Lu Yu, who specialized in the functions of tea.

Lu Yu was an orphan and he grew up in a temple. He used to chop firewood in the mountains when he was very young and this caused him to have minor cuts and scratches on his hands all the time. His legs were also always swollen with boils due to insect bites. Fortunately, an old man who chopped firewood for a living always helped him by cleaning the wounds using diluted tea, and bandaging them with a layer of mashed tea leaves applied to the wounds. The wounds healed quickly with this treatment.

While looking for firewood one day, Lu Yu ate some wild fruit and started vomiting and had diarrhea after that. Once again, the old man took care of him by feeding him a bowl of boiled tea leaves and mustard flowers. Lu Yu recovered immediately after drinking the soup. Lu Yu began to find tea fascinating because of this and he decided to write a book to introduce the medicinal value and properties of tea to the world so that people might understand tea, love it, and use it to improve their health.

It was not until he began to research on tea when he found that the available documented materials were very limited. He then went to the regions which had tea plantations to study tea properties, its cultivation methods, and production process. In A. D. 760, Lu Yu settled down in a dilapidated temple in Huzhou with all the researched materials he had collected on tea and began to write his book. Four years later, he finished writing the *Book of Tea* (*cha jing*), the first book in China to contain a detailed and comprehensive record of the functions and information of tea.

The book was extremely popular among the people and it greatly promoted the cultivation and production of tea, Lu Yu was eventually accorded the title of the God of Tea as a result of the success of the *Book of Tea*.

Culture of the Tea

In China, tea has a long history of 3,000 years. At the 7th century (during the Sui and Tang Dynasty), tea became the indispensable drink for every family's daily life. Later, teahouses appeared in cities, where friends could talk with each other or watch performances and listen to the stories while drinking tea. The teahouse is a good place to relax oneself or to hold a friend-party. And it is a Chinese custom to serve the guest a cup of tea.

Tea is a kind of healthy drink. It tastes moderate and does good to refreshing oneself, helping digest and diuresis. As a result, Chinese often drink tea to keep fit. People also often hold tea parties or drink tea instead of wine at the dinner to g am in a healthy way.

Moreover, Chinese philosophy demonstrates the culture of the tea, too. It is said that the Chinese people are just like tea, who are always sober and reasonable towards the world, who propose harmony, helping and relying on each other in the social life. Gentle, moderate and understanding are the features of the culture of the tea.

第八課

李春造橋

中國河北省有座古橋叫趙州橋，是一千多年前隋朝石匠李春設計的。

李春出生在河北趙州，父親是個瓦匠。他從小跟著父親學習技術，非常努力，還常常向老師傅請教。

李春的故鄉趙州城南5里地，有一條大河叫洨(xiáo)河，每到夏秋兩季雨水很大，給兩岸百姓帶來許多不便。人們希望建造一座又牢固又方便行船的大橋。這件事在當時來說是很困難的。因為橋

趙州橋

要牢固就要有橋墩，而有了橋墩就不方便行船。李春想了很久，他想到：建房屋常用拱形結構，建橋為什麼不能用呢？他設計了一個單孔拱形石橋，橋體兩邊各開兩個小橋洞。平時河水從大橋洞流過，發大水時河水還可以從四個小橋洞流過。這樣減少了流水對橋身的沖力，橋就不容易被水沖壞，同時還減輕了橋的重量，節省了石料。

趙州橋全長50.8米，寬9.6米，而橋的高度只有7米，所以橋面平緩，無論車馬還是行人過橋都不吃力。拱形還使橋身看上去十分美觀，被人們比做一彎新月和雨後長虹。

一千三百多年過去了，經過了無數次的風雨、洪水和地震，這座古橋至今完好地橫跨在洨河上，每天迎接著過往的車馬行人。

生詞

qiáo 橋	bridge	shè jì 設計	design
suí cháo 隋朝	Sui Dynasty	róng yì 容易	easy
wǎ jiang 瓦匠	bricklayer	jié shěng 節省	save
qǐng jiào 請教	consult	píng huǎn 平緩	(of slopes, etc.) gentle
láo gù 牢固	secure; solid	měi guān 美觀	aesthetic
qiáo dūn 橋墩	bridge pier	wān 彎	crescent
gǒng xíng 拱形	arch	zhì jīn 至今	up to now
jié gòu 結構	structure		

聽寫

橋　彎　牢固　平緩　設計　至今　美觀

容易　節省　請教　*瓦匠　結構

比一比

$\begin{cases} 拱（拱形）\\ 洪（洪水）\end{cases}$　　$\begin{cases} 彎（彎曲）\\ 灣（台灣）\end{cases}$　　$\begin{cases} 緩（平緩）\\ 暖（溫暖）\end{cases}$

近義詞

美觀——好看　　不便——麻煩　　節省——節約

反義詞

加——減　　加重——減輕　　緩——急

直——彎　　困難——容易

詞語運用

設計　建造

李春設計了趙州橋。

李春和眾多的工匠一起建造了趙州橋。

彩虹　紅色

雨後，空中出現了一道美麗的彩虹。

太陽是紅色的還是金色的？

判斷對錯

1. 趙春設計了趙州橋。　　　　　　　　　　　　　___對___錯

2. 趙州橋已經存在1030年了。　　　　　　　　　　___對___錯

3. 趙州橋的橋體兩邊各開了兩個小橋洞。　　　　　___對___錯

4. 李春設計的是一個雙孔拱形石橋。　　　　　　　___對___錯

Lesson Eight

Li Chun and the Zhaozhou Bridge

There is an ancient bridge located in Hebei Province which is known as the Zhaozhou Brige. It was designed by a stonemason named Li Chun during the Sui Dynasty more than 1,000 years ago.

Li Chun was born in Zhaozhou City, Hebei Province. His father was a bricklayer. Li Chun was very hardworking and started learning the professional bricklayering skills from his father and other experienced and skilled workers from a young age.

At that time, there was a big river, the Xiao River, located five li (approximately 2,500meters) to the south of Zhaozhou City, where Li Chun lived. During the rainy seasons in summer and autumn, the flood from the river would cause great inconvenience to the people living at the riverbank. The locals planned to construct a huge and stable bridge over the river to facilitate river crossing, and yet to ensure that the bridge will not block the navigation route. This was a challenging task at that time because constructing a firmly secure bridge required piers, which would inevitably block the water way. Li Chun thought about it for a long time and the structure of a house provided him with inspiration. He thought, "Is it possible that the arch structure commonly used in building houses be applied to constructing a bridge as well?" He then designed an arch stone bridge with a big opening in the middle, and two smaller ones on each side. This design allows the river to flow through the big opening on normal days and the additional four small openings at the sides will further facilitate the flow of the swollen river during the rainy seasons. This design greatly reduced the impact of rushing water on the body of the bridge when it flooded, thus making the bridge more secure. Furthermore, because of the openings in the bridge, the entire construction would not require as much concrete and stone.

The Zhaozhou Bridge is 50.8 meters in length, 9.6 meters in width, and only 7 meters in height. The bridge surface is smooth and even, and the gradient of the slope is gentle. Wagons and pedestrians travel on it without much difficulty. The unique arch shape also has an aesthetic effect and it reminds people of a crescent or a rainbow.

More than 1,300 years have passed and the ancient bridge has survived numerous thunderstorms, floods, and earthquakes. Today it is still standing across the Xiao River, welcoming wagons and pedestrians.

第九課

"藥王"孫思邈

隋唐時期，中國醫學有了很大發展。唐朝皇帝唐太宗很重視醫學，開辦了科目分得比較細的醫學校。

唐代有位著名的醫學家、藥物學家孫思邈。他從小就對醫學有興趣，二十來歲時已成了有名的醫生。他很關心病人，對窮苦的病人，不但看病不要錢，還把藥送給他們。

孫思邈（公元581年—682年）

一次，有個病人排不出尿，找到孫思邈，哀求他："救救我吧，我的肚子快要脹破了，實在受不了啦！"孫思邈看完他的病，認為吃藥已經來不及了，得想辦法先把尿液引出來。他正在著急，忽然看到一個小孩在吹蔥管玩，蔥管前面尖，中間空，這不是天然的導尿管嗎？他把蔥管切去尖的一頭，小心地插進病人的尿道裏，再用力一吸，果然尿液順著蔥管流了出來。病人得救了。孫思邈成了世界上第一個給病人導尿的人。

又有一次，他在路上看見四個人抬著一口棺材，從棺材裏滴出了鮮血。他急忙上前問是怎麼一回事。一位老婆婆哭著說："我女兒生小孩，兩天兩夜沒生下來，就死了。"孫思邈從地上沾了一點血，看了一會兒說："從這血看不像是真死，讓我試試看。"於是大家把棺材打開，孫思邈一看那婦人臉上已沒有一點血色，仔細摸摸脈，還有一點跳動。他趕忙選定穴位，給病人扎針。不一會兒，產婦醒過來了，孩子也生出來了。一針救了兩條命。

有一個病人腿疼，吃了好多中藥也沒有好。孫思邈給他針灸，扎了好幾針，病人還是一直喊疼。孫思邈想，除了前人用過的365個穴位外，難道沒有別的穴位了嗎？他決心嘗試一下，尋找新穴位。他一邊用手輕輕按病人身上不同的部位，一邊問病人疼不疼。突然病人大叫一聲："啊……是，是這裏疼。"孫思邈就在這個點上扎針。不一會

明代針灸銅人，通高213厘米，全身有666個針灸點

兒，病人的腿疼止住了。後來，用這種方法找到的新穴位就被稱為"阿是"穴。

孫思邈注意到山裏的窮人有一種怪病，白天眼睛好好的，到了傍晚就像麻雀一樣，什麼也看不見了。他想：為什麼有錢人不得這種病呢？看來這個病是因為窮人身體內缺少了什麼營養引起的。他認為窮人吃肉和動物肝髒很少，就叫病人多吃動物肝髒。沒多久，這些病人夜裏就能看見東西了。原來，夜盲眼是食物中缺少維生素A引起的，而動物肝髒裏有較多的維生素A。

不過，孫思邈又發現，有錢人雖然沒有夜盲眼，可是常常得腳氣病。他想這也很可能和吃的東西有關。不知窮人吃了什麼東西，富人沒有吃到。他發現窮人吃粗糧多，粗糧含有米糠(kāng)和麥麩(fū)，而富人吃的細糧中都沒有。於是他讓病人吃米糠和麥麩，不久，真的把腳氣病治好了。

老年孫思邈將一生行醫的經驗寫成了《千金方》一書。書中記載了800多種藥物和5000多個藥方。人們尊敬地稱他為"藥王"。

生詞

zhòng shì 重視	pay attention to		zhēn jiǔ 針灸	acupuncture and moxibustion
kē mù 科目	subject		máng 盲	blind
bǐ jiào 比較	compare		quē shǎo 缺少	lack; be short of
pái niào 排尿	urinate		wéi shēng sù 維生素	vitamins
zhàng 脹	be bloated		hán yǒu 含有	constitutes
cōng 葱	green Chinese onion; scallion		jīng yàn 經驗	experience
guān cai 棺材	coffin		jì zǎi 記載	record
dī 滴	dripping		zūn jìng 尊敬	respect
xué wèi 穴位	acupoint			

聽寫

重視　排尿　脹　比較　含有　缺少　維生素

經驗　尊敬　科目　*穴位　葱

比一比

素 { 維生素 / 素菜 }　　敬 { 敬禮 / 尊敬 }　　{ 交（交換）/ 較（比較）/ 校（學校）}

詞語運用

重視　重量

在美國的學校裏，大家都很重視體育運動。

曹操想知道大象的重量。

興趣　高興

我對下棋很有興趣。

如果你幫助了別人，你會感到很高興。

婦人　富人

大樹下坐著一位婦人和一個孩子。

醫生發現富人容易得糖尿病。

判斷對錯

1. 宋代有位著名的醫學家、藥物學家叫孫思邈。　　___對___錯

2. 孫思邈是世界上第一個給病人導尿的人。　　___對___錯

3. 有一次孫思邈一針救了兩條人命。　　___對___錯

4. "阿是"穴是孫思邈發現的。　　___對___錯

5. 孫思邈是個很愛動腦筋的人。　　___對___錯

 English Translation

Lesson Nine

Sun Simiao, the King of Medicine

It was during the Sui Dynasty and the Tang Dynasty when Chinese traditional medical science developed rapidly. The second emperor of the Tang Dynasty emphasized greatly on the development of medical science and had even sponsored a medical school to research different areas of specializations.

There was a famous expert in Chinese traditional medicine and pharmacology during the Tang Dynasty and his name was Sun Simiao. His interest in medical science started since his childhood. Sun became a famous doctor in his early 20s. He cared a lot for his patients and would provide free diagnosis and medicines at his clinic for poor patients.

There was once a patient who had not been able to urinate came to Sun, begging him: "Please help me. My belly is going to burst. I can't bear with it any longer." Sun diagnosed him and thought that it was too late for the patient to take any medicine and that the pressing thing to do then was to draw out his urine. While he was thinking intensely about the problem, Sun saw a kid blowing into a straw of spring onion. The spring onion had a pointed end and was hollow inside. It suddenly occurred to Sun that this was the perfect natural urinary catheter. He immediately cut the pointed end of the green onion and put it carefully into the patient's urethra. After a single suction, the urine was drawn out along the green onion. The patient was saved and Sun became the inventor of urethral catheterization. He

was the first person in the world to use the technique.

On another occasion, Sun came across four people carrying a coffin on the road and noticed that there was blood dripping from the coffin. He went up immediately and asked them what had happened. An old woman who was weeping, said: "My daughter went into labor for two whole days; but her baby wasn't delivered and she died." Sun examined the blood that had dripped on the ground for a while and said, "Judging from the blood, she is probably still alive. Let me take a look." So the people opened the coffin and the face of the woman was as pale as death. Sun felt her pulse carefully and he perceived a faint beating. He quickly determined an acupuncture point and inserted a needle. After a while, the woman came round and she delivered her baby. Sun managed to save two lives with one needle.

There was yet another incident where the patient had been suffering from an acute pain in the legs. He had taken many types of medicines and yet none of them worked for him. Sun Simiao treated him using acupuncture. But after administering several needles, the patient still felt the pain. Sun considered the 365 acupuncture points founded by the ancestors, and wondered if there were more points to be discovered. He was determined to attempt to locate the points that were yet to be discovered. He gently pressed on different parts of the patient's body, asking him at the same time where the pain was coming from. Suddenly, the patient shouted, "Ah… yes. That is the spot." Sun applied a needle to that very spot and the pain in the patient's legs ceased. From then on, he named the acupuncture point he discovered as "Ah-shi", meaning "Ah… yes!" point.

On another occasion, Sun noticed that some people living in the mountainous area were suffering from a queer disease. These patients were able to see well during the day, but when night came, they could see nothing in the evening, just like sparrows. He thought about the disease and wondered, "Why are the rich people not suffering from this kind of disease? The disease must be caused by a lack in certain nutrients in the body. He observed that the poor were consuming inadequate amount of meat and organs like liver, and he recommended his patients to eat more of these food items. It didn't take too long before his patients regained their sight at night. And now we know that the disease, nyctalopia, or night blindness, is caused by a lack of Vitamin A in the diet, and animal liver is rich source of Vitamin A.

Although the rich did not have night blindness, Sun noticed that many of them suffered from a disease known as beriberi. Again, he believed that this had something to do with the people's diet. So he paid special attention to the food that the poor ate which the rich didn't. He soon found that the poor ate foods that were coarse and high in fibre, containing rice husk and wheat bran. The rich, however, ate mainly refined flour and rice that did not contain that much fibre. Accordingly, he prescribed the bran to the rich patients and that cured their beriberi successfully.

Sun summarized his life-long experience in medical practice in a book entitled *Prescriptions Worth Thousands in Gold* (*qian jin fang*), which recorded more than 800 types of medicine and over 5,000 prescriptions. The Chinese people gave him the respected title "King of Medicine".

第十課

李時珍和他的《本草綱目》

李時珍（1518年—1593年）是明朝著名的醫藥學家。

李時珍出生在湖北一個醫生家庭。他的父親希望他好好讀書，長大當官。可是李時珍從小就喜愛醫學，24歲那年正式當了醫生。他對病人熱情，看病十分認真，很快就出名了。

李時珍（公元1518年—1593年）

有一年，他的家鄉湖北大旱，因為沒有水，衛生差，生病的人很多。找他看病的許多窮人沒有錢，他還是給他們治病。李時珍救治了無數病人，名聲越來越大。後來明朝皇帝讓他到宮裏當了醫官。可是他不喜歡這個工作，不想當一個沒有作為的只給皇帝看病的醫生。一年以後，他就離開皇宮回到家鄉去了。

李時珍行醫的時候讀了很多醫藥書籍，發現書中有不少錯誤，他決心寫一部比較完善的藥物著作。於是，他走訪了長江、黃河流域的湖北、湖南、江西、江蘇、河北，還有廣東、廣西等許多地方，採集藥材。看到一些不知道名稱的植物，他就採下來，向當地的老百姓請教，弄明白這種植物的生長特性和用途，然後記錄下來。完成了多年的走訪之後，李時珍返回家鄉，他又查閱了前人的800多種醫藥書籍，認真做好筆記。經過27個春秋的努力，1578年他終於寫成了藥物學巨著——《本草綱目》。

《本草綱目》這部書內容非常豐富，共52卷，收入了1892種能治病的藥物，藥方一萬多個，插圖一千多幅。全書約190萬字，文字優美又有哲學道理。閱讀《本草綱目》，你會感到李時珍對生命的尊重和治病救人的善良心願。從17世紀起，《本草綱目》被翻譯成日、德、英、法、俄等多國文字，成為世界醫藥學的重要文獻。

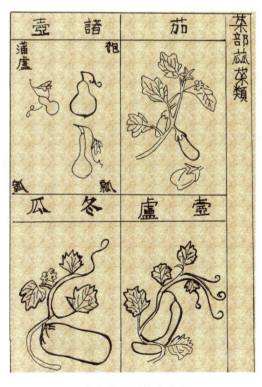

《本草綱目》插圖

生詞

jiā tíng 家庭	family	chá yuè 查閱	look up
zhèng shì 正式	formal; official	gāng mù 綱目	compendium
wèi shēng 衛生	hygiene	nèi róng 內容	content
shū jí 書籍	books	juàn 卷	volume
cuò wù 錯誤	mistake	yōu měi 優美	graceful; beautiful
wán shàn 完善	perfect; comprehensive	zhé xué 哲學	philosophy
zhù zuò 著作	works; writings	fān yì 翻譯	translate
cǎi jí 採集	collect	é wén 俄文	Russian (language)
nòng 弄	cause to	zhòng yào 重要	important; significant
yòng tú 用途	functions; purpose	wénxiàn 文獻	literature; written record
jì lù 記錄	note down; record		

聽寫

家庭　正式　衛生　書籍　著作　內容　錯誤

閱　優美　重要　用途　弄

比一比

衛 { 衛生 / 保衛 }　　翻 { 翻譯 / 翻開 }　　途 { 用途 / 路途 }

容 { 內容 / 容易 }　　卷 { 第一卷 / 卷子 }　　聲 { 名聲 / 聲音 }

反義詞

錯誤——正確　　差——好　　熱情——冷淡

詞語運用

正式　　各式各樣

去年李雷的姐姐正式工作了。

商店裏擺(bǎi)著各式各樣的水果。

衛生　　衛士

大家都要講衛生，不要往地上亂扔東西。

國王和他的衛士很快上了船。

容易　　內容

想在足球比賽中得第一，可不是一件容易的事。

這本書的內容十分豐富。

判斷對錯

1. 李時珍是明朝著名的醫藥學家。　　　　　　　　＿＿對＿＿錯

2. 李時珍治病認真，對病人熱情，給許多窮人治病，很快就出名了。　　　　　　　　　　　＿＿對＿＿錯

3. 李時珍當過皇帝的醫官。他喜歡這個工作。　　　＿＿對＿＿錯

4. 李時珍發現許多醫書中有錯誤，他決心寫一部完善的藥物著作。　　　　　　　　　　　　＿＿對＿＿錯

5. 李時珍經過23年的努力，寫成了藥物學巨著。　　＿＿對＿＿錯

6. 《本草綱目》是世界醫藥學的重要文獻。　　　　＿＿對＿＿錯

Lesson Ten

Li Shizhen and His Compendium of Materia Medica

Li Shizhen (1518-1593) was a famous doctor and pharmacologist during the Ming Dynasty.

He was born in a doctor's family in Hubei Province. His father encouraged him to study hard to secure an official post when he grew up. But Li loved medical science and became a doctor when he turned 24. As he was a warm and careful doctor, he soon became popular among the people.

One year, his hometown suffered severe drought and many fell ill due to a lack of water and poor hygiene. Some of his patients were poor and could not afford the treatment but he treated them all the same. His fame spread even farther after he had saved numerous patients and even the emperor invited him to be a medical official in the imperial palace. However Li disliked the job as he did not want to remain a doctor solely for the emperor's service hence he resigned one year later to return to his hometown.

During his professional career as a doctor, Li discovered a lot of mistakes in the medical books he came across. He was determined to write a more comprehensive and accurate book on medicines. In order to do that, Li traveled to the regions around the Yangtze River and the Yellow River, visiting Hubei, Hunan, Jiangxi, Jiangsu, Hebei, and other places like Guangdong and Guangxi, to gather herbs with medicinal value. Whenever he spotted an unknown plant, he would ask the locals about it and record the information about its properties and functions. After many years of traveling, Li returned to his hometown and he researched and read over more than 800 medical books written before his time. As he read, Li took notes carefully. After 27 years of hard work, he finally finished his masterpiece in pharmacology entitled the Compendium *of Materia Medica* (*ben cao gang mu*).

The *Compendium of Materia Medica* is extremely rich in content, consisting of 52 volumes, recording 1,892 curative medicines, more than 10,000 prescriptions and over 1,000 illustrations. The book contains 1,900,000 beautifully scripted characters and is full of philosophical thoughts. When one reads the compendium, one would be able to sense the appreciation Li had for life and his compassion for the sick. The book has been translated into Japanese, German, English, French, and Russian since the 17th century. It is often referred to and known as an important source of pharmacological literature in the world.

第十一課

都江堰

在中國四川省成都附近，有一個聞名世界的水利工程，叫都江堰（dū）。它是2000多年前，戰國時期李冰修建的。論年歲，它比長城還要老，可是兩千多年後的今天，長城早已成為古跡，而都江堰卻像個年輕人不分晝夜地工作著，灌溉著成都平原的幾百萬畝良田。

都江堰建成以前，岷江時常發洪水，當地人民生活很苦。

有一年，李冰被派到四川成都做官。他到那裏後，聽說岷江水災很厲害，就想把岷江的水治好。他同當地百姓沿著岷江，從下游到上游，察看地形，瞭解水情，終於找到了水災的原因。

都江堰

原來，岷江發源於岷山。每年春天，山上的雪化了，雪水就從四面八方流進岷江。到了平原，岷江河道變窄，江水就漲到岸

都江堰全景

上,把莊稼淹了。

李冰決定在岷江剛進入平原的地方,把江水一分為二,一股水沿原來的老河床流走;另一股水通過開的新河道,流向成都平原灌溉田地。這實在是一個好辦法。

但是,要開一條新河道十分困難,一座玉壘山擋住了江水去成都平原的路。李冰決定把山劈開。動工的時候,漫山遍野響起了斧鑿的聲音,叮叮噹噹,十分熱鬧。但是山石很硬,不容易被鑿開。李冰讓人用柴草把石頭燒熱,再潑上冷水,石頭就裂開了。經過大家7年多艱苦的勞動,終於把山鑿開了一個20米寬的大口子,人們叫它寶瓶口。

新河道開好了,但是岷江的水,只有很少一部分流入新河道。原因是新河道這一邊的地勢比較高,流到這邊來的江水自然就少。怎麼辦呢?

寶瓶口

李冰決定在岷江中築一道"分水堤"，逼著江水更多地流入寶瓶口。要在江心築一道堤，可不容易。開始，他們用泥土和鵝卵石壘了一道分水堤，可是沒過幾天，就被江水沖垮了。後來又用大石塊築了一道比較牢固的大堤，誰知道一漲大水，大堤又被沖垮了。李冰整天想怎麼樣築堤才不會被水沖垮這個問題。

李冰父子塑像

一天，他看到山上到處長著竹子，又看見婦女在小河裏放了一些竹籠，裏邊泡著要洗的衣服，儘管河水流得很急，竹籠卻沖不走。於是李冰想出了一個好主意。他讓人們編了好多大竹籠，裏邊裝滿鵝卵石，再把竹籠一排排地沉到江裏去，果然，江水沖不走它們了。這樣，一道幾里長的牢固的分水堤，終於建成了。岷江的水被分成了兩股，其中的一股就乖乖地流進了寶瓶口。從此以後，岷江再也沒有鬧過水災，老百姓過上了安寧、幸福的生活。人們在都江堰東邊建了一座廟紀念李冰。

第十一課

生詞

dū jiāng yàn 都江堰	Dujiang Weir	lěi 壘	a structure built with piled bricks, stones, etc.
shuǐ lì gōngchéng 水利工程	water conservancy project or works		
zhǔ chí 主持	preside over; be responsible for	pō shuǐ 潑水	sprinkle water
guàn gài 灌溉	irrigate	jiān kǔ 艱苦	arduous
mǔ 畝	a Chinese unit of area	píng 瓶	bottle
mín jiāng 岷江	Minjiang River	dī 堤	dyke; dam
zāi 災	disaster	bī 逼	force
zhǎi 窄	narrow	chōng kuǎ 沖垮	break down
zhǎng 漲	swell after absorbing water	pào 泡	steep; soak
zhuāng jia 莊稼	crops	guāi 乖	obedient; without deviating
gǔ 股	a unit of measurement for flowing water	jì niàn 紀念	commemorate

聽寫

窄　畝　災　漲　莊稼　逼　水利工程　潑水

紀念　艱苦　瓶　*堤

65

中國古代科學技術

比一比

{ 家（家庭）
  稼（莊稼）

{ 難（困難）
  艱（艱苦）

{ 服（衣服）
  股（股票）

{ 堤（大堤）
  提（提高）

反義詞

寬——窄　　　漲——落　　　硬——軟

多音字

都(dū)

都(dū) { 成都
        都江堰

都(dōu)

都(dōu) { 都是
         都行

詞語運用

近　　進

新華書店離學校很近。

鈴響了，同學們急忙走進教室上課。

火災　水災

樹林裏容易發生火災，人人都要小心。

沒有建造都江堰的時候，岷江常常鬧水災。

張開　上漲

小鳥張開嘴等著鳥媽媽餵它。

連下幾天大雨，河水上漲了一米。

一股

還沒有走到廚房，我就聞到一股烤肉的香味。

山腳下有一股泉水。

閱讀

神奇的都江堰

都江堰是世界上最古老的無壩(bà)引水工程。它位於四川岷江中游，是戰國時期李冰修建的。讓人驚嘆的是，2000多年來它一直很好地工作，造福成都平原。

都江堰水利工程主要由魚嘴、飛沙堰和寶瓶口三部分組成。

魚嘴是個分水堤，它把岷江分為外江和內江。外江河床寬，是原來的老河道；內江是新河道，用於引水灌溉。這樣，水少的季節，岷江60％的水會流入內江灌溉田地；而洪水季節，60％水會順著外江的河道流走。魚嘴還利用了彎道流體力學的原理，使表層水流入內江，而含泥沙多的底層水流向外江，於是大部分沙石就留在外江河道裏。

　　飛沙堰是內江上一個不高的水堤，它高出內江河床2.15米。當內江的水量太大，寶瓶口流不過去的時候，多餘的水會越過飛沙堰流走；如果有大洪水的時候，它還會自行潰(kuì)堤，江水又會流回岷江。

都江堰示意圖

　　寶瓶口在玉壘山上，是內江流向成都平原的入水口。它是人工開鑿的，只有20米寬。內江水從百米寬的河道流向寶瓶口時，河道變窄，水流加快。到了洪水季節，由於飛沙堰的調節，寶瓶口入水不會過量，成都平原可以安全灌溉。

四川人民為了紀念李冰，修了一座廟，每年農曆六月還有廟會活動。

Lesson Eleven

The Dujiang Weir

The Dujiang Weir is a world famous water conservancy project located near Chengdu, Sichuan Province. Constructed more than 2,200 years ago, the Dujiang Weir was designed by Li Bing during the Warring States Period. It still stands today and continues to irrigate several million mu (the unit of measurement is equivalent to 0.16 acres) of fertile farmland on the Chengdu Plain.

Before the construction of the weir, the locals who lived along the Minjiang River suffered great losses caused by floods which occurred each time the river swelled.

A year came when Li Bing was delegated to Chengdu to serve as a local official. Upon his arrival, Li realized that the locals suffered a lot from the frequent floods and resolved to change the situation. He traveled along the Minjiang River with some locals, starting from the lower reaches all the way to the upper reaches in order to familiarize himself with the land forms and the current. After inspecting the area for some time, he finally found the reason behind the flood.

It turned out that the Minjiang River originated from Mount Min and at the end of every spring, the snow melted and flowed down from the mountain into the river. When the river reaches the plain, the course is much narrower and this causes the water to rise above the banks, flooding the farmlands.

Li Bing decided to divide the river into two streams at the point when it entered the plain, allowing one course to run along the original river course, while channeling another course along a newly constructed river so that it can irrigate the farmland on the Chengdu Plain. This was a truly brilliant idea.

But it was difficult to construct a new river course, because the Yulei Mountain blocked the course flow to the Chengdu Plain. Li Bing had no choice but to dig a tunnel in the mountain. The sounds of chopping and chiseling could be heard far and wide. But the rocks were too hard and could not be chopped. Li Bing then instructed the laborers to burn the rocks using firewood, and then to splash cold water on them as the rocks will be easier to break after that. After seven years of hard labor, a large 20 meters wide hole was finally dug. The gap was called the Bottleneck.

Although a new river course had been constructed, only a small amount of river water could flow into the course, because the ground around the new course was relatively higher compared to that of the original river course. In order to solve the problem, Li Bing decided to construct a diversion levee in the middle of the Minjiang River to channel more water into the Bottleneck. But again, it was a difficult task. Firstly, they tried to construct it using soil and pebbles; but it stood for only several days before it was shattered by the water. They then constructed a more secure levee using big stones; but this levee too, could not withstand the pressure of the flood. "What could they do next?" This was the only question Li Bing had his mind.

One day, he noticed that there were bamboo forests all over the mountain. He also noticed some women lowering bamboo cages into the river to soak the clothes inside before washing. Although the river current was rapid, it could not carry the cages away. Upon seeing this, Li had an idea. He asked for labor to weave large bamboo cages, filled them with pebbles and sank the cages in rows into the river. As expected, the river current could not sweep the cages away and a secure diversion levee of more than several li (the unit of measurement is equivalent to 500 meters) long was finally constructed. The Minjiang River is now divided into two streams, one of which gently flows into the Bottleneck. From then on, people living along the Minjiang River never suffered from floods again and they led peaceful, happy lives. The people built a temple to the east of the Dujiang Weir to commemorate and show their gratitude to Li Bing.

The Mirable Dujiang Weir

The Dujiang Weir is the earliest river diversion project in the world to be carried out without constructing dams. It is located along the middle reaches of the Minjiang River in Sichuan Province and the entire construction process was led by Li Bing of the Warring States period. For more than 2,000 years now, the Dujiang Weir continues to function to serve the people of the Chengdu Plain.

The Dujiang Weir project consisted of three parts known as the Yuzui, the Feisha Weir, and the Bottleneck.

The Yuzui is a diversion levee which divides the Minjiang River into two; where there is an outer river course and an inner river course. The river bed of the outer course is quite wide and the water runs along the original river course. The inner course is formed by the new river course and this course is used for channeling and irrigation. 60% of all the river water will flow into the inner course to irrigate the farmland during the dry season. And during the flooding season, the excess water would flow out to the outer river course. The hydrodynamic theory has also been applied here. This ensures that as the surface water flows deeper into the inner river course, the muddy water near the bottom of the bed is channeled to the outer stream. As a result, most sand and scree are left in the outer stream.

The Feisha Weir is a levee in the inner river course, which is only 2.15 metres higher than the riverbed of the inner river. When the water of the inner river overflows or does not flow through the Bottleneck, the water will run over the Feisha Weir. Once there are strong floods, the Feisha Weir can automatically break down in order to allow the water to return to the Minjiang River.

The Bottleneck is the entrance to the inner course which runs towards the Chengdu Plain. It was manually excavated through the Yulei Mountain and is only 20 meters wide. So when the water runs along a 100 meters wide river course to the Bottleneck, the river course narrows down, causing the stream current to speed up. Even if it were the flooding season, water running through the Bottleneck will not be overwhelming because of the adjustments made to Feisha Weir. This ensures that the Chengdu Plain will always be irrigated.

In order to commemorate Li Bing, the people of Sichuan Province built a temple and hold fairs in the temple in June every year, as according to the lunar calendar.

第十二課

中國瓷器

談起瓷器，人們就會想到中國。"中國"一詞在英語中是"China"，就是瓷器的意思。不錯，瓷器是中國人發明的，中國是瓷器的故鄉。

自從瓷器進入人類的生活，算起來已經有1800多年了。現在我們的日常生活幾乎離不開瓷器。比如廚房裏的瓷盤、瓷碗、瓷壺、瓷杯，客廳裏的瓷花瓶、瓷臺燈，衛生間（廁所）裏的抽水馬桶、瓷洗澡盆，蓋房子用的瓷磚、瓷瓦，還有精美的瓷器藝術品。除了日常生活之外，工業上也需要瓷器，像飛機、航天飛行器使用的耐高溫、高硬度的材料等等。

陶瓶（距今約6500年—5000年）

那麼中國人是怎樣發明瓷器的呢？回答這個問題還要先從陶器說起。

早在6000年前，中國人就會製造陶器了。陶器是用泥土做成盆、碗、罐等形狀，再放到火裏燒成的。陶器表面粗糙，吸水性強，也比較脆。

唐三彩（公元618年—公元907年）

4000年前，中國人燒製出了一種漆黑光亮的黑陶。黑陶很美，壁很薄，有的黑陶的壁像蛋殼一樣薄，讓人驚嘆！

到了3000年前（商朝），中國人又發明了"原始青瓷"。瓷器是用泥土做胎，在胎上塗上一層釉，再放到1200度的高溫中燒製而成。瓷器比陶器堅硬，外表光亮好看，不吸水或很少吸水，又方便清洗。這些優點是陶器所沒有的。

1800年前（東漢）真正的青瓷終於燒製出來了。到這時，瓷器才算誕生了。在青瓷之後，中國人又燒出了白瓷和彩瓷。青瓷的表面是淡

北宋（公元960年—公元1127年）

淡的綠色或黃色，看上去像美玉；而白瓷，潔白如雪。白瓷的出現，在瓷器發展的歷史上是一件很重要的事，因為有了白瓷，才可以在瓷器表面畫出美麗的圖畫。

13世紀（元朝），中國的彩瓷多起來了。彩瓷中最有名的是青花瓷。青花瓷白底藍花，那藍色的圖畫很像中國的水墨畫。青花瓷一出現就受到了人們的喜愛。

早在7世紀（唐朝），中國的瓷器就通過絲綢之路運到了西方。後來唐朝又開通了從廣州到波斯灣的航線，中國瓷器又能從海上銷往中東和歐洲。

12世紀（宋朝），中國瓷器發展到了輝煌的時期。中國瓷已銷到日本、朝鮮、印度等五十多個國家。那時候瓷器貿易盛況空前。雖然精美的中國瓷器價格很高，但還是供不應求。來自各國的商船在泉州港進進出出，十分熱鬧。一艘又一艘的商船把中國的瓷器運到了世界各地。

元青花（公元1279年—公元1368年）

生詞

cí qì 瓷器	china	qī hēi 漆黑	jet-black
chú fáng 廚房	kitchen	yuán shǐ 原始	primitive
kè tīng 客廳	living room	tāi 胎	roughcast (*in the making of China, etc.*)
cè suǒ 廁所	toilet; bathroom	yòu 釉	glaze
chōu shuǐ mǎ tǒng 抽水馬桶	flush toilet; water closet	jiān yìng 堅硬	hard; durable
gài 蓋	build ; cover	yōu diǎn 優點	merits; advantages
cí zhuān 瓷磚	ceramic tile	dàn shēng 誕生	be born; come into existence
xū yào 需要	require	háng xiàn 航線	air or shipping line
táo qì 陶器	pottery	xiāo 銷	sell
cuì 脆	brittle	jià gé 價格	price

聽寫

瓷器　廚房　客廳　廁所　堅硬　優點　誕生

價格　蓋房　需要　航線

比一比

{ 次（一次）
  瓷（瓷器）

{ 消（消息）
  銷（銷售）

{ 專（專家）
  轉（轉動）

{ 乎（幾乎）
  呼（呼吸）

{ 傳（傳說）
  轉（轉動）

{ 抬（抬著）
  胎（胎兒）

反義詞

漆黑——雪白　　　柔軟——堅硬

優點——缺點　　　誕生——死亡

多音字

幾 jī
幾乎

幾 jǐ
幾個

詞語解釋

供不應求——提供的東西不能滿足需要。

盛況空前——從來沒有過的盛大、熱鬧的場面。

判斷對錯

1. 瓷器是中國人發明的，中國是瓷器的故鄉。　　　＿＿對＿＿錯
2. 6000年前，中國人已會燒製陶器。　　　　　　＿＿對＿＿錯
3. 4000年前，中國人燒製出了壁像蛋殼
   一樣薄的黑陶。　　　　　　　　　　　　　　＿＿對＿＿錯
4. 陶器比瓷器堅硬，光亮好看。　　　　　　　　＿＿對＿＿錯
5. 1800年前，青瓷燒製出來，瓷器誕生了。　　　＿＿對＿＿錯
6. 彩瓷中最有名的是青花瓷。青花瓷很美。　　　＿＿對＿＿錯
7. 古代，中國瓷器只能從海上銷往中東和歐洲。　＿＿對＿＿錯
8. 12世紀（宋朝），中國瓷器已銷往五十多
   個國家。　　　　　　　　　　　　　　　　　＿＿對＿＿錯

小知識

景德鎮

　　位於江西省的景德鎮是中外著名的瓷都，早在漢代就開始生產陶瓷。從1004年開始，很長的時間裏，那裏專門燒製宮廷(tíng)用的陶瓷。那裏的工匠曾燒出無數精美的瓷器。人們都說景德鎮瓷器"白如玉、薄如紙、明如鏡"。

 English Translation

Lesson Twelve

Chinese China

When referring to china, or porcelain, people would inevitably associate it with the country, China. The country's name, China, in English, refers to "china". Porcelain, or china, was indeed invented by the Chinese and China is its country of origin.

It has been 1,800 years when humans first started using china in their daily lives. Today, we can hardly do without china. For instance, we use porcelain cutlery and crockery in the kitchen and dining room. We place porcelain vases and porcelain reading lamps in the living room. In the bathroom (toilet), we have flush toilets and porcelain bathtubs. When building houses, we use ceramic tiles and other fine porcelain artwork. Besides daily life items, porcelain is also used in industrial areas as it is heat-resistant and durable. These are the properties that qualify it to be materials for various equipments in airplanes or space crafts.

So how did the Chinese invent china? To answer this question, we should begin with pottery.

Earlier than 6,000 years ago, the Chinese learned to make pottery, which initially was clay that was heated in the furnace and shaped into pots, bowls, and jars. A work of pottery has a rough coat which absorbs a lot of water, causing it to be brittle.

4,000 years ago, the Chinese produced black pottery, which was pitch-black in color and had a beautiful sheen to it. Its layer was quite thin, and some were even as thin as eggshells, which was really quite incredible.

During the Shang Dynasty which was about 3,000 years ago, the Chinese invented the "original celadon porcelain" which also had a clay surface. In order to make it, it was to be coated with a layer of glaze first and then heated in a high temperature of 1,200 degrees. Compared to pottery, porcelain is harder. It also has a shiny and pretty coat, and does not absorb too much water. This makes it more convenient to clean the porcelain. Pottery do not have these advantages.

During Eastern Han Dynasty 1,800 years ago, people made real celadon porcelain. It was during this period of time when china was born. After inventing the celadon porcelain, the Chinese forged white porcelain as well as other colorful porcelain. The coat of the celadon porcelain was light green or yellow, like the color of jade; while the white porcelain was as white as the snow. It was very important in history of porcelain development that people could forge white porcelain, because beautiful pictures could then be drawn on its surface.

In the 13th century, during the Yuan Dynasty, more and more colorful porcelain entered the market. Qing-hua porcelain was the most famous among them. It had blue flower patterns on its white background and the blue floral patterns looked like Chinese ink. People always loved Qing-hua porcelain the moment they lay their eyes on it.

During the Tang Dynasty in the 7th century, china was transported to the west through the Silk Road. Later on, when the shipping line was opened in the Tang Dynasty to connect Guangzhou to Persian Gulf, china could also be sold to people in the Middle East and Europe.

During the Song Dynasty in the 12th century, the development of porcelain reached its Golden Age. The china of China was sold to more than 50 countries like Japan, Korea, India, and so on. At that time, the porcelain trade was an unprecedented one. Although the price of porcelain was very high, the supply of fine china from China was not meeting up with the demand for it. Many boats from different countries came and left the Quanzhou Port, which eventually became a bustling town. Each ship that entered the port took these goods made by China to various places in the world, spreading the fame of China products far and wide.

生字表（繁）

1. 磁(cí) 勺(sháo) 薄(báo) 凹(āo) 鋼(gāng) 配(pèi) 羅(luó) 霧(wù) 初(chū) 促(cù)

2. 蔡(cài) 倫(lún) 帛(bó) 絮(xù) 糙(cāo) 繭(jiǎn) 棍(gùn) 綿(mián) 揭(jiē) 舊(jiù) 驗(yàn) 漿(jiāng) 墨(mò) 宜(yí) 阿(ā)

3. 爆(bào) 煉(liàn) 銅(tóng) 爐(lú) 炸(zhà) 炭(tàn) 例(lì) 混(hùn) 未(wèi) 武(wǔ) 末(mò) 槍(qiāng) 彈(dàn) 供(gōng)

4. 抄(chāo) 速(sù) 雕(diāo) 版(bǎn) 畢(bì) 坊(fáng) 匠(jiàng) 膠(jiāo) 稿(gǎo) 蠟(là) 壓(yā) 拆(chāi)

5. 衡(héng) 仰(yǎng) 距(jù) 祖(zǔ) 測(cè) 震(zhèn) 演(yǎn) 渾(hún) 儀(yí) 製(zhì) 洛(luò) 隴(lǒng)

6. 紡(fǎng) 墓(mù) 式(shì) 紋(wén) 裙(qún) 側(cè) 袍(páo) 轟(hōng) 蒜(suàn) 蘿(luó) 蔔(bo) 葡(pú) 萄(táo) 詳(xiáng) 置(zhì)

7. 專(zhuān) 寺(sì) 敷(fū) 瀉(xiè) 湯(tāng) 介(jiè) 紹(shào) 查(chá)

8. 橋(qiáo) 隋(suí) 瓦(wǎ) 牢(láo) 墩(dūn) 拱(gǒng) 構(gòu) 計(jì) 緩(huǎn) 彎(wān)

9. 較(jiào) 尿(niào) 脹(zhàng) 蔥(cōng) 棺(guān) 滴(dī) 穴(xué) 灸(jiǔ) 盲(máng) 缺(quē) 素(sù) 含(hán) 載(zǎi)

10. 庭(tíng) 籍(jí) 誤(wù) 弄(nòng) 錄(lù) 閱(yuè) 綱(gāng) 卷(juàn) 優(yōu) 哲(zhé) 譯(yì) 俄(é)

中國古代科學技術

11. 堰 持 溉 畝 岷 災 窄 漲 莊 稼 壘 艱 瓶 堤
    逼 垮 泡 乖

    （yàn chí gài mǔ mín zāi zhǎi zhǎng zhuāng jià lěi jiān píng dī
     bī kuǎ pào guāi）

12. 瓷 廚 廁 抽 蓋 磚 需 陶 脆 漆 胎 釉 堅 誕
    銷 價

    （cí chú cè chōu gài zhuān xū táo cuì qī tāi yòu jiān dàn
     xiāo jià）

共計155个生字

生字表（简）

1. 磁(cí) 勺(sháo) 薄(báo) 凹(āo) 钢(gāng) 配(pèi) 罗(luó) 雾(wù) 初(chū) 促(cù)

2. 蔡(cài) 伦(lún) 帛(bó) 絮(xù) 糙(cāo) 茧(jiǎn) 棍(gùn) 绵(mián) 揭(jiē) 旧(jiù) 验(yàn) 浆(jiāng) 墨(mò) 宜(yí) 阿(ā)

3. 爆(bào) 炼(liàn) 铜(tóng) 炉(lú) 炸(zhà) 炭(tàn) 例(lì) 混(hùn) 未(wèi) 武(wǔ) 末(mò) 枪(qiāng) 弹(dàn) 供(gōng)

4. 抄(chāo) 速(sù) 雕(diāo) 版(bǎn) 毕(bì) 坊(fáng) 匠(jiàng) 胶(jiāo) 稿(gǎo) 蜡(là) 压(yā) 拆(chāi)

5. 衡(héng) 仰(yǎng) 距(jù) 祖(zǔ) 测(cè) 震(zhèn) 演(yǎn) 浑(hún) 仪(yí) 制(zhì) 洛(luò) 陇(lǒng)

6. 纺(fǎng) 墓(mù) 式(shì) 纹(wén) 裙(qún) 侧(cè) 袍(páo) 轰(hōng) 蒜(suàn) 萝(luó) 卜(bo) 葡(pú) 萄(táo) 详(xiáng) 置(zhì)

7. 专(zhuān) 孤(gū) 寺(sì) 敷(fū) 泻(xiè) 汤(tāng) 介(jiè) 绍(shào) 查(chá) 者(zhě)

8. 桥(qiáo) 隋(suí) 瓦(wǎ) 牢(láo) 墩(dūn) 拱(gǒng) 构(gòu) 计(jì) 缓(huǎn) 弯(wān)

9. 较(jiào) 尿(niào) 胀(zhàng) 葱(cōng) 棺(guān) 滴(dī) 穴(xué) 灸(jiǔ) 盲(máng) 缺(quē) 素(sù) 含(hán) 载(zǎi)

10. 庭(tíng) 籍(jí) 误(wù) 弄(nòng) 录(lù) 阅(yuè) 纲(gāng) 卷(juàn) 优(yōu) 哲(zhé) 译(yì) 俄(é)

中國古代科學技術

11. 堰(yàn) 持(chí) 溉(gài) 亩(mǔ) 岷(mín) 灾(zāi) 窄(zhǎi) 涨(zhǎng) 庄(zhuāng) 稼(jià) 垒(lěi) 艰(jiān) 瓶(píng) 堤(dī)
逼(bī) 垮(kuǎ) 泡(pào) 乖(guāi)

12. 瓷(cí) 厨(chú) 厕(cè) 抽(chōu) 盖(gài) 砖(zhuān) 需(xū) 陶(táo) 脆(cuì) 漆(qī) 胎(tāi) 釉(yòu) 坚(jiān) 诞(dàn)
销(xiāo) 价(jià)

共計155個生字

生詞表（繁）

1. 磁(cí) 勺(sháo) 自由(zì yóu) 薄(báo) 凹(āo) 指示(zhǐ shì) 鋼(gāng) 配(pèi) 方位(fāngwèi) 羅盤(luó pán) 霧(wù)
   迷失(mí shī) 初(chū) 促進(cù jìn) 航海(háng hǎi)

2. 蔡倫(cài lún) 竹簡(zhú jiǎn) 笨重(bènzhòng) 報告(bàogào) 帛(bó) 貴(guì) 絲絮(sī xù) 粗糙(cū cāo) 蠶繭(cán jiǎn) 棍子(gùn zi)
   絲綿(sī mián) 揭(jiē) 生產(shēng chǎn) 舊(jiù) 漁網(yú wǎng) 破布(pò bù) 原料(yuánliào) 試驗(shì yàn) 漿(jiāng)
   墨(mò) 便宜(pián yi) 阿拉伯(ā lā bó)

3. 火藥(huǒ yào) 煙花(yānhuā) 爆竹(bàozhú) 煉(liàn) 青銅(qīngtóng) 爐(lú) 爆炸(bàozhà) 木炭(mù tàn) 按照(ànzhào)
   比例(bǐ lì) 混合(hùn hé) 前所未有(qiánsuǒwèiyǒu) 力量(lì liang) 武器(wǔ qì) 末(mò) 槍(qiāng) 子彈(zǐ dàn) 供(gōng)

4. 印刷(yìnshuā) 抄寫(chāo xiě) 速度(sù dù) 雕版(diāobǎn) 作坊(zuōfang) 工匠(gōngjiàng) 下棋(xià qí) 膠泥(jiāo ní)
   稿件(gǎojiàn) 蠟(là) 壓(yā) 拆下(chāixia)

5. 張衡(zhāng héng) 珍珠(zhēnzhū) 仰(yǎng) 距離(jù lí) 祖先(zǔ xiān) 北斗星(běi dǒuxīng) 測定(cè dìng) 地震(dì zhèn)
   演示(yǎn shì) 渾天儀(húntiān yí) 天文學(tiān wénxué) 製造(zhì zào) 洛陽(luòyáng) 隴西(lǒng xī)

6. 紡織(fǎng zhī) 墓(mù) 各式各樣(gè shì gèyàng) 花紋(huāwén) 裙子(qún zi) 側(cè) 絲袍(sī páo) 光彩奪目(guāngcǎi duó mù)

83

中國古代科學技術

	hōng dòng	jìn fàn	jì xù	rè qíng	jiǔ xí	dà suàn	hú luó bo	pú táo
	轟動	進犯	繼續	熱情	酒席	大蒜	胡蘿蔔	葡萄
	xiáng xì	wèi zhì	fēng sú	jiē dài	jiāo liú			
	詳細	位置	風俗	接待	交流			

	zhuān jiā	gū ér	sì yuàn	huá pò	dǎo làn	fū	shàng tù xià xiè	tāng
7.	專家	孤兒	寺院	劃破	搗爛	敷	上吐下瀉	湯
	jiè shào	chá zhǎo	zī liào	liǎo jiě	tè xìng	zhòng zhí	jiā gōng	zuò zhě
	介紹	查找	資料	瞭解	特性	種植	加工	作者

	qiáo	suí cháo	wǎ jiang	qǐng jiào	láo gù	qiáo dūn	gǒng xíng	jié gòu	shè jì
8.	橋	隋朝	瓦匠	請教	牢固	橋墩	拱形	結構	設計
	róng yì	jié shěng	píng huǎn	měi guān	wān	zhì jīn			
	容易	節省	平緩	美觀	彎	至今			

	zhòng shì	kē mù	bǐ jiào	pái niào	zhàng	cōng	guān cai	dī	xué wèi	zhēn jiǔ
9.	重視	科目	比較	排尿	脹	蔥	棺材	滴	穴位	針灸
	máng	quē shǎo	wéi shēng sù	hán yǒu	jīng yàn	jì zǎi	zūn jìng			
	盲	缺少	維生素	含有	經驗	記載	尊敬			

	jiā tíng	zhèng shì	wèi shēng	shū jí	cuò wù	wán shàn	zhù zuò	cǎi jí
10.	家庭	正式	衛生	書籍	錯誤	完善	著作	採集
	yòng tú	jì lù	chá yuè	gāng mù	nèi róng	juàn	yōu měi	zhé xué
	用途	記錄	查閱	綱目	內容	卷	優美	哲學
	fān yì	é wén	zhòng yào	wén xiàn				
	翻譯	俄文	重要	文獻				

	dū jiāng yàn	shuǐ lì gōng chéng	zhǔ chí	guàn gài	mǔ	mín jiāng	zāi zhǎi
11.	都江堰	水利工程	主持	灌溉	畝	岷江	災窄
	zhǎng	zhuāng jia	gǔ	lěi	pō shuǐ	jiān kǔ	píng	dī	bī	chōng kuǎ	pào
	漲	莊稼	股	壘	潑水	艱苦	瓶	堤	逼	沖垮	泡
	guāi	jì niàn						
	乖	紀念						

12. 瓷器(cí qì)　廚房(chú fáng)　客廳(kè tīng)　廁所(cè suǒ)　抽水馬桶(chōushuǐ mǎtǒng)　蓋(gài)　瓷磚(cízhuān)　需要(xū yào)

陶器(táo qì)　脆(cuì)　漆黑(qī hēi)　原始(yuánshǐ)　胎(tāi)　釉(yòu)　堅硬(jiānyìng)　優點(yōudiǎn)　誕生(dàn shēng)

航線(hángxiàn)　銷(xiāo)　價格(jià gé)

共計212個生詞

生詞表（簡）

1. 磁(cí) 勺(sháo) 自由(zì yóu) 薄(báo) 凹(āo) 指示(zhǐ shì) 钢(gāng) 配(pèi) 方位(fāngwèi) 罗盘(luó pán) 雾(wù) 迷失(mí shī) 初(chū) 促进(cù jìn) 航海(háng hǎi)

2. 蔡伦(cài lún) 竹简(zhú jiǎn) 笨重(bènzhòng) 报告(bàogào) 帛(bó) 贵(guì) 丝絮(sī xù) 粗糙(cū cāo) 蚕茧(cán jiǎn) 棍子(gùn zi) 丝绵(sī mián) 揭(jiē) 生产(shēng chǎn) 旧(jiù) 渔网(yú wǎng) 破布(pò bù) 原料(yuánliào) 试验(shì yàn) 浆(jiāng) 墨(mò) 便宜(pián yi) 阿拉伯(ā lā bó)

3. 火药(huǒyào) 烟花(yānhuā) 爆竹(bàozhú) 炼(liàn) 青铜(qīngtóng) 炉(lú) 爆炸(bàozhà) 木炭(mù tàn) 按照(ànzhào) 比例(bǐ lì) 混合(hùn hé) 前所未有(qiánsuǒwèiyǒu) 力量(lì liang) 武器(wǔ qì) 末(mò) 枪(qiāng) 子弹(zǐ dàn) 供(gōng)

4. 印刷(yìnshuā) 抄写(chāoxiě) 速度(sù dù) 雕版(diāobǎn) 作坊(zuōfang) 工匠(gōng jiàng) 下棋(xià qí) 胶泥(jiāo ní) 稿件(gǎojiàn) 蜡(là) 压(yā) 拆下(chāi xia)

5. 张衡(zhāng héng) 珍珠(zhēnzhū) 仰(yǎng) 距离(jù lí) 祖先(zǔ xiān) 北斗星(běi dǒuxīng) 测定(cè dìng) 地震(dì zhèn) 演示(yǎn shì) 浑天仪(hún tiān yí) 天文学(tiān wénxué) 制造(zhì zào) 洛阳(luòyáng) 陇西(lǒng xī)

6. 纺织(fǎngzhī) 墓(mù) 各式各样(gè shì gèyàng) 花纹(huāwén) 裙子(qún zi) 侧(cè) 丝袍(sī páo) 光彩夺目(guāngcǎi duó mù)

生詞表

| hōngdòng | jìn fàn | jì xù | rè qíng | jiǔ xí | dàsuàn | hú luó bo | pú táo |
| 轰动 | 进犯 | 继续 | 热情 | 酒席 | 大蒜 | 胡萝卜 | 葡萄 |

xiángxì　wèi zhì　fēng sú　jiē dài　jiāo liú
详细　位置　风俗　接待　交流

7. zhuān jiā　gū ér　sì yuàn　huá pò　dǎo làn　fū　shàngtù xià xiè　tāng
专家　孤儿　寺院　划破　捣烂　敷　上吐下泻　汤

jièshào　chá zhǎo　zī liào　liǎo jiě　tè xìng　zhòngzhí　jiā gōng　zuò zhě
介绍　查找　资料　了解　特性　种植　加工　作者

8. qiáo　suícháo　wǎjiang　qǐngjiào　láo gù　qiáodūn　gǒngxíng　jié gòu　shè jì
桥　隋朝　瓦匠　请教　牢固　桥墩　拱形　结构　设计

róng yì　jié shěng　pínghuǎn　měiguān　wān　zhì jīn
容易　节省　平缓　美观　弯　至今

9. zhòngshì　kē mù　bǐ jiào　páiniào　zhàng　cōng　guān cai　dī　xuéwèi　zhēnjiǔ
重视　科目　比较　排尿　胀　葱　棺材　滴　穴位　针灸

máng　quē shǎo　wéishēng sù　hányǒu　jīngyàn　jì zǎi　zūnjìng
盲　缺少　维生素　含有　经验　记载　尊敬

10. jiā tíng　zhèngshì　wèishēng　shū jí　cuò wù　wán shàn　zhù zuò　cǎi jí
家庭　正式　卫生　书籍　错误　完善　著作　採集

nòng　yòngtú　jì lù　cháyuè　gāngmù　nèiróng　juàn　yōuměi　zhéxué
弄　用途　记録　查阅　纲目　内容　卷　优美　哲学

fān yì　é wén　zhòngyào　wén xiàn
翻译　俄文　重要　文献

11. dū jiāng yàn　shuǐ lì gōng chéng　zhǔ chí　guàngài　mǔ　mínjiāng　zāi　zhǎi
都江堰　水利工程　主持　灌溉　亩　岷江　灾　窄

zhǎng　zhuāng jia　gǔ　lěi　pō shuǐ　jiān kǔ　píng　dī　bī　chōngkuǎ　pào
涨　庄稼　股　垒　泼水　艰苦　瓶　堤　逼　冲垮　泡

guāi　jì niàn
乖　纪念

87

中國古代科學技術

12. 瓷器 厨房 客厅 厕所 抽水马桶 盖 瓷砖 需要

陶器 脆 漆黑 原始 胎 釉 坚硬 优点 诞生

航线 销 价格

共计212个生词

第二課

一　寫生詞

蔡	倫											
帛												
絲	絮											
粗	糙											
蠶	繭											
棍	子											
絲	綿											
揭												
舊												
試	驗											
漿												
墨												

便	宜								
阿	拉	伯							

二 組詞

笨_____　　棍_____　　破_____　　驗_____

料_____　　繭_____　　阿_____　　墨_____

網_____　　術_____　　揭_____　　糙_____

舊_____　　漿_____　　繭_____　　宜_____

三 選字組詞

（絲　思）想　　出（使　便）　　破（布　巾）

（絲　思）綢　　（使　便）宜　　毛（布　巾）

洗（驗　臉）　　（揭　渴）開　　（敲　高）門

試（驗　臉）　　口（揭　渴）　　（敲　高）興

四 寫出反義詞

方便——　　薄——　　光滑——

便宜——　　新——　　笨重——

五 變換偏旁組成新字,再組詞

驗—— (　　)　　　揭—— (　　)

粗—— (　　)　　　織—— (　　)

六 根據課文判斷對錯

1. 古代沒有紙,人們把字寫在竹簡上。竹簡很輕,也很方便。　　＿＿對＿＿錯

2. 古時候,只有有錢人纔用帛寫字。　　＿＿對＿＿錯

3. 蔡倫用樹皮、麻頭、舊漁網和破布造紙。　　＿＿對＿＿錯

4. 蔡倫造紙試驗了許多次。　　＿＿對＿＿錯

5. 蔡倫造的紙又輕又便宜又好用。　　＿＿對＿＿錯

6. 公元 105 年蔡倫把這一重大發明報告給皇帝。　　＿＿對＿＿錯

7. 造紙術在幾百年后傳到了世界各地。　　＿＿對＿＿錯

8. 造紙術只促進了中國文化的發展。　　＿＿對＿＿錯

七 造句

1. 便宜＿＿＿＿＿＿＿＿＿＿＿＿＿＿＿＿＿＿＿＿

2. 方便＿＿＿＿＿＿＿＿＿＿＿＿＿＿＿＿＿＿＿＿

八　根據課文回答問題（請寫出一個完整的句子）

1. 中國古代還沒有發明紙的時候，人們把字寫在什麼東西上面？

   答：_____

   _____

2. 紙和竹簡哪一個寫字更方便、好用？

   答：_____

   _____

九　朗讀課文三遍

第四課

一　寫生詞

抄	寫											
速	度											
雕	版											
畢												
作	坊											
工	匠											
膠	泥											
稿	件											
蠟												
壓												
拆	下											

二 組詞

刷____　　版____　　硬____　　匠____

壓____　　棋____　　整____　　稿____

膠____　　拆____　　抄____　　速____

三 選字組詞

出（板　版）　　下（其　棋）　　（整　正）齊

軟（硬　更）　　（其　棋）他　　（整　正）在

（壓　廠）平　　（稿　高）山　　雕（刻　該）

工（壓　廠）　　（稿　高）子　　應（刻　該）

四 寫出反義詞

簡單——　　　　　　　整齊——

堅硬——

五 根據課文填空

1. 中國古代在印刷術發明以前，書要一個字一個字地用手_____，速度很慢。

2. 雕版印刷比起用手抄寫,不知快了多少。但是每塊雕版上的字都是_____在一起的,每換一次內容,就得重刻一次版,很不_____。

3. 一次,畢昇和朋友下棋。下著下著,他看看棋盤又看看棋子,突然想:"如果印刷版上的字像_____一樣,變成活的,那多好啊!"

六 選擇填空(請把詞語寫在空白處)

1. 這本書是什麼時候_____的?(出版　木板)

2. 院子裏的_____牆上有一隻小松鼠在吃果子。

(出版　木板)

3. 王華_____下得很好。(下棋　星期)

4. _____五下午沒課。(星期　下棋)

5. 我要把這個禮物親手_____媽媽。(膠泥　交給)

七 根據課文判斷對錯

1. 在印刷術發明以前,書要一個字一個字地用手抄寫。　　　　　___對___錯

2. 雕版印刷,是用刀把字刻在硬木上,再印刷。　　　　　　　　　　　　　　　____對____錯

3. 北宋人畢昇發明了活字印刷術。　____對____錯

4. 畢昇小時候在一家做鞋的作坊當工匠。____對____錯

5. 畢昇和朋友下棋時想了一個好主意。____對____錯

6. 畢昇在膠泥上刻字,再用火燒硬,這就成了"活"字。　　　　　　　　　　　____對____錯

7. 活字印刷術使印書又快又簡單。____對____錯

8. 印刷術后來傳到朝鮮、日本、阿拉伯和歐洲。　　　　　　　　　　　　　　____對____錯

八 縮寫課文(至少寫八句話)

_____

_____

_____

_____

_____

_____

九　朗讀課文三遍

第六課

一 寫生詞

紡	織										
墓											
花	紋										
裙	子										
側											
絲	袍										
轟	動										
大	蒜										
胡	蘿	蔔									
葡	萄										
詳	細										
位	置										

各式各樣

二 組詞

紡____　訪____　蒜____　詳____

葡____　墓____　蘿____　羅____

紋____　裙____　式____　試____

側____　轟____　袍____　置____

三 填字組詞

(　)軟美麗　　各(　)各樣　　十分(　)奇

美麗非(　)　技術發(　)　(　)產絲綢

華麗(　)比　　光彩(　)目　　全場(　)動

四 選字組詞

(紡　訪)織　　考(試　式)　　(紋　蚊)子

(紡　訪)問　　(試　式)樣　　花(紋　蚊)

(裙　群)子　　長(袍　包)　　山(詳　羊)

一(裙　群)　　書(袍　包)　　(詳　羊)細

五 根據課文選擇正確答案

1. 漢武帝時，第一次派_____出使西域。

   A 曹操　　　　　B 張騫(qiān)

2. 張騫_____就被匈奴抓住了。

   A 走到西域　　　B 走到半路

3. 張騫逃出來，經過草原、沙漠終於到了_____。

   A 漢朝　　　B 歐洲　　　C 西域

4. 張騫_____西域各國的情況，並寫成文字報告給皇帝。

   A 詳細地考察了　　　B 吃了一頓酒席就瞭解了

5. 公元前123年，漢武帝派兵打敗了_____。

   A 匈奴　　　　　B 日本

六 根據課文判斷對錯

1. 早在五六千年前，中國人就用蠶絲織成絲綢做衣服穿。　　　____對____錯

2. 絲綢的衣服美麗，可是不柔軟。　　　____對____錯

3. 到了唐宋時期，絲織品已是美麗非凡。　　　____對____錯

4. 唐代織造的一種薄綢，兩面都有花紋，還能透過光線。　　　　　　　　　　　　　　____對____錯

5. 唐代還會用鳥的羽毛織裙子。　　____對____錯

6. 據說，古羅馬的凱撒(kǎi sā)大帝穿過中國的絲袍。　　　　　　　　　　　　　　____對____錯

七　造句

1. 熱情_____

2. 繼續_____

3. 各式各樣_____

八　根據課文回答問題(請寫出完整的句子)

1. 為什麼中國被稱為"絲綢之國"？

_____

_____

2. 中國從什麼時候就開始養蠶了？

_____

_____

九 縮寫課文第二部分第一段（至少寫六句話，"鶩"字可以寫拼音）

十 朗讀課文三遍

第八課

一　寫生詞

橋												
隋	朝											
瓦	匠											
牢	固											
橋	墩											
拱	形											
結	構											
設	計											
緩												
彎												

二 組詞

州＿＿＿　　洲＿＿＿　　瓦＿＿＿　　牢＿＿＿

橋＿＿＿　　減＿＿＿　　拱＿＿＿　　構＿＿＿

緩＿＿＿　　計＿＿＿　　技＿＿＿　　彎＿＿＿

三 選字組詞

結（構　溝）　　（瓦　瓶）匠　　（供　拱）形

水（構　溝）　　（瓦　瓶）子　　提（供　拱）

（瀉　寫）字　　資（料　斗）　　（孤　狐）兒

四 寫出反義詞

彎──　　　減──　　　容易──

緩──

五 寫出近義詞

美觀──　　　　　節省──

六 根據課文填空

1. 趙州橋是一千多年前隋朝石匠＿＿＿＿＿＿＿＿設計的。

2. 李春設計了一個＿＿＿＿＿＿＿＿拱形石橋，橋體兩邊各開＿＿＿＿＿＿＿＿個小橋洞。

七 詞語解釋

1. 請教＿＿＿＿＿＿＿＿＿＿＿＿＿＿＿＿＿＿＿＿＿＿＿＿＿＿＿＿＿＿＿

2. 吃力＿＿＿＿＿＿＿＿＿＿＿＿＿＿＿＿＿＿＿＿＿＿＿＿＿＿＿＿＿＿＿

八 根據課文判斷對錯

1. 中國河北省有座一千多年前隋朝建的古橋叫趙州橋。　　　＿＿對＿＿錯

2. 趙州橋是石匠李春設計的。　　　＿＿對＿＿錯

3. 李春的父親是個建築師。　　　＿＿對＿＿錯

4. 趙州橋是單孔拱形石橋，方便行船。　　　＿＿對＿＿錯

5. 趙州橋橋體兩邊各開四個小橋洞。　　　＿＿對＿＿錯

6. 趙州橋橋面平緩，無論車馬行人過橋，都不吃力。　　　＿＿對＿＿錯

7. 一千三百多年過去了，這座古橋至今完好地在使用。　　　＿＿對＿＿錯

九 造句

1. 設計＿＿＿＿＿＿＿＿＿＿＿＿＿＿＿＿＿＿＿
2. 節省＿＿＿＿＿＿＿＿＿＿＿＿＿＿＿＿＿＿＿

十 簡單介紹一下趙州橋（至少寫七句話）

＿＿＿＿＿＿＿＿＿＿＿＿＿＿＿＿＿＿＿＿＿＿＿
＿＿＿＿＿＿＿＿＿＿＿＿＿＿＿＿＿＿＿＿＿＿＿
＿＿＿＿＿＿＿＿＿＿＿＿＿＿＿＿＿＿＿＿＿＿＿
＿＿＿＿＿＿＿＿＿＿＿＿＿＿＿＿＿＿＿＿＿＿＿
＿＿＿＿＿＿＿＿＿＿＿＿＿＿＿＿＿＿＿＿＿＿＿
＿＿＿＿＿＿＿＿＿＿＿＿＿＿＿＿＿＿＿＿＿＿＿

十一 朗讀課文三遍

第十課

一 寫生詞

家	庭											
書	籍											
錯	誤											
弄												
記	錄											
查	閱											
綱	目											
卷												
優	美											
哲	學											
翻	譯											
俄	文											

二 組詞

式____ 優____ 庭____ 善____

記____ 籍____ 譯____ 誤____

閱____ 容____ 衛____ 獻____

三 選字組詞

（熱 熟）人　　清（旱 早）　　日（記 紀）

（熱 熟）鬧　　乾（旱 早）　　世（記 紀）

四 近義詞填空

喜歡　仔細　停止　許多　不夠

缺少——（　　　）　　好多——（　　　）

停住——（　　　）　　喜愛——（　　　）

認真——（　　　）

五 寫出反義詞

正確——　　　冷淡——　　　差——

六 選擇填空（請把詞語寫在空白處）

1. 李時珍是明朝著名的＿＿＿＿＿＿。

（醫藥學家　天文學家）

2. 李時珍寫成了藥物學巨著＿＿＿＿＿＿。

（《西遊記》　《本草綱目》）

3.《本草綱目》收入了＿＿＿＿多個醫方。（一千　一萬）

4.《本草綱目》收入了＿＿＿＿種能治病的藥物。

（1892　892）

七 根據課文選擇正確答案（把答案寫在空白處）

1. 李時珍對病人＿＿＿＿，看病十分認真，很快就出名了。

　A 冷淡　　　　　B 熱情

2. 有一年，湖北大旱，因為沒有水，＿＿＿＿差，生病的人很多。

　A 衛生　　　　　B 衛士

3. 李時珍發現醫藥書籍中有不少錯誤，決心寫一部比較＿＿＿＿的藥物著作。

　A 完全　　　　　B 完善

4.《本草綱目》這部書_____非常豐富。

    A 形容　　　　　　　B 內容

5. 從17世紀起,《本草綱目》被譯成多國文字,成為世界醫藥學的_____文獻。

    A 重要　　　　　　　B 主要

八 造句

1. 優美_____
2. 重要_____
3. 衛生_____

九 縮寫課文《李時珍和他的〈本草綱目〉》(至少寫八句話)

_____

_____

_____

_____

_____

十　朗讀課文三遍

第十二課

一 寫生詞

瓷器											
廚房											
廁所											
蓋											
瓷磚											
需要											
陶器											
脆											
漆黑											
胎											
釉											
堅硬											
誕生											

銷											
價	格										
抽	水	馬	桶								

二　組詞

瓷_____　　廚_____　　廁_____　　磚_____

誕_____　　需_____　　價_____　　蓋_____

抽_____　　堅_____　　優_____　　客_____

三　選字組詞

一（次　瓷）　　（傳　磚）說　　舞（臺　胎）　　價（各　格）

瓷（哭　器）　　（專　磚）家　　（危　脆）險

四　反義詞填空

堅硬　　缺點　　死亡　　雪白

漆黑——（　　）　　　　　　柔軟——（　　）

優點——（　　）　　　　　　誕生——（　　）

五　選擇填空（請把詞語寫在空白處）

1. 衛生間就是_____。（廚房　廁所）

2. 青花瓷瓶是_____。（瓷器　陶器）

3. 小紅有個_____，就是吃東西前洗手。（優點　缺點）

4. 絲綢的衣服很_____。（堅硬　柔軟）

5. 那時精美的中國瓷器_____很高。（價格　用途）

六　根據課文選擇正確答案（請把答案寫在空白處）

1. 瓷器走進人類生活，已有_____的歷史了。

　　A 18000 多年　　　B 180 多年　　　C 1800 多年

2. 在 4000 年前，中國人燒製出了一種漆黑光亮的_____。

　　A 青花瓷　　　　B 黑陶　　　　C 青瓷

3. 彩瓷中最有名的是白底藍花的_____。

　　A 青花瓷　　　　B 陶器

4. 12 世紀（宋朝），各國的商船把中國的瓷器運到了_____。

　　A 世界各地　　　B 上海　　　　C 長城

七 根據課文判斷對錯

1. "China"一詞原意就是瓷器。　　　　　___對___錯

2. 瓷器是中國人在1800年前發明的。　　　___對___錯

3. 瓷器比陶器出現得早。　　　　　　　　___對___錯

4. 彩瓷中最有名的是青花瓷。青花瓷白底藍花。　　　　　　　　　　　　　　　___對___錯

5. 12世紀(宋朝)中國瓷器發展到了輝煌的時期。　　　　　　　　　　　　　　　___對___錯

八 縮寫課文《中國瓷器》(至少寫十句話)

_____
_____
_____
_____
_____
_____
_____
_____

九 朗讀課文三遍

第二課聽寫

第四課聽寫

第六課聽寫

第八課聽寫

第十課聽寫

第十二課聽寫

練習紙

中國古代科學技術

第一課

一　寫生詞

磁												
勺												
薄												
凹												
鋼												
配												
羅盤												
霧												
初												
促進												

二 組詞

磁_____　勺_____　氣_____　汽_____

迷_____　米_____　促_____　捉_____

霧_____　初_____　鋼_____　自_____

羅_____　薄_____　發_____　航_____

三 選字組詞

（氣　汽）車　　（航　船）海　　（米　迷）路

（促　足）球　　（促　足）進　　打（雷　霧）

四 選詞填空

航海業　放在　歐洲　羅盤　2000　1000　小船　磨

1. 大約在_____多年前的戰國時期，中國人就發明了指南針。

2. 在_____多年前，中國人又發明了"指南魚"。

3. "指南魚"魚肚部分凹下去一些，放在水面可以像_____一樣浮起來。

4. 人工磁化的方法，就是把鐵片與天然磁石_____一起緊緊地挨著，時間久了，鐵片就有了磁性。

5. 人們把一根鋼針放在磁石上_____，使鋼針變成了磁針。

6. 12世紀中國的海船上就裝有_____。這樣不管是白天還是黑夜，陰雨還是大霧，船都不會迷失方向，使海上航行安全多了。

7. 13世紀初，中國的指南針傳到_____，大大促進了世界_____的發展。

五 選擇填空（請把詞語寫在空白處）

1. 中國最早的指南針叫_____。（司機　司南）

2. 這幾天，許多航空_____的票都減價了。
piào　jià

（司機　公司）

3. 如果你在野外旅行，最好帶上指南針，這樣纔不會_____。

（米飯　迷路）

六 造句

不管……還是……_____

七 詞語解釋

1. 發明＿＿＿＿＿＿＿＿＿＿＿＿＿＿＿＿＿＿

2. 促進＿＿＿＿＿＿＿＿＿＿＿＿＿＿＿＿＿＿

八 根據課文回答問題（請寫出完整的句子）

1. 指南針是歐洲人發明的還是中國人發明的？什麼時候發明的？

答：＿＿＿＿＿＿＿＿＿＿＿＿＿＿＿＿＿＿
＿＿＿＿＿＿＿＿＿＿＿＿＿＿＿＿＿＿＿＿

2. 船在海上航行，靠什麼指方向？

答：＿＿＿＿＿＿＿＿＿＿＿＿＿＿＿＿＿＿
＿＿＿＿＿＿＿＿＿＿＿＿＿＿＿＿＿＿＿＿

九 朗讀課文三遍

第三課

一　寫生詞

爆	竹										
煉											
青	銅										
爐											
爆	炸										
木	炭										
比	例										
混	合										
武	器										
末											
槍											
子	彈										

供										
前	所	未	有							

二 組詞

炭____ 混____ 爆____ 例____

供____ 煉____ 末____ 武____

炸____ 混____ 彈____ 槍____

三 選字組詞

（炸 昨）天　　（未 末）年　　戰（爭 淨）

爆（炸 昨）　　（未 末）有　　乾（爭 淨）

比（列 例）　　（促 足）進　　（混 棍）合

排（列 例）　　（促 足）球　　（混 棍）子

四 寫出反義詞

增強——　　　　　初——

五 選擇填空（請把詞語寫在空白處）

1. 春節是中國人最重要的_____。（節日　節目）

2. 美麗的煙花和爆竹是用_____製成的。

（絲綢　火藥）

3. 火藥是中國人_____多年前發明的。（1500　500）

4. 火藥可以用來開山_____。（採礦　採花）

5. 下完雨,天上出現了一道_____。（採礦　彩虹）

6. 有了火藥,人類得到了一種巨大的_____。

（力量　重量）

7. 公元1225年至1284年間,火藥傳入印度,以後又傳入阿拉伯和_____。（美洲　歐洲）

六 詞語解釋

前所未有_____

七 根據課文判斷對錯

1. 火藥是中國人最早發明的。　　　　____對____錯

2. 漢代，中國人就發現木炭和硫磺(liú huáng)混在一起
　　會爆炸。　　　　　　　　　　　　　　　　＿＿對＿＿錯

3. 有了火藥後，很快火藥就被用在武器上。　　＿＿對＿＿錯

4. 唐朝末年，中國人發明了火藥箭。　　　　　＿＿對＿＿錯

5. 火藥還可以開山採礦，做成煙花和爆竹。　　＿＿對＿＿錯

八　根據閱讀材料《勇敢的萬户》判斷對錯

1. 第一個"坐"火箭的萬户是明朝人。　　　　　＿＿對＿＿錯

2. 萬户想飛上高高的天空。　　　　　　　　　＿＿對＿＿錯

3. 萬户坐在安裝了火箭的椅子上，每隻
　　手裏拿著一個大風箏。　　　　　　　　　　＿＿對＿＿錯

4. 萬户成功了，他飛上了天空。　　　　　　　＿＿對＿＿錯

5. 萬户很勇敢。　　　　　　　　　　　　　　＿＿對＿＿錯

九　朗讀課文三遍

第五課

一 寫生詞

張	衡											
仰												
距	離											
祖	先											
測	定											
地	震											
演	示											
渾	天	儀										
製	造											
洛	陽											
隴	西											

二 組詞

仰_____　　迎_____　　顆_____　　棵_____

仔_____　　距_____　　祖_____　　演_____

震_____　　測_____　　製_____　　渾_____

三 選字組詞

（粗　祖）先　　（仔　子）細　　（混　渾）天儀

（粗　祖）細　　兒（仔　子）　　（混　渾）合

（距　巨）大　　地（震　霧）

（距　巨）離　　下（震　霧）

四 組新字

1. 木—果（　　）　　　2. 果—頁（　　）

五 填上適當的形容詞

　　　　紅紅的　美麗的　綠色的　無邊的

　　白白的　閃閃的　寒冷的　炎熱的　黑色的

（　　　）星星　　（　　　）花朵　　（　　　）夜空

（　　　）太陽　　（　　　）草地　　（　　　）冬天

（　　　）雪花　　（　　　）大海　　（　　　）夏天

六 根據課文填空

1. 張衡小時候能數_____顆星星。

2. 爺爺走過來說："孩子,你看得很_____。天上的星星是在動,可是,它們之間的_____是不變的。"

七 選擇填空（請把詞語寫在空白處）

1. 張衡是東漢時期偉大的_____。（天文學家　軍事家）

2. 媽媽說："快把地裏的玉米_____!"

　　　　　　　　　　　　　　　　（數一數　數學）

3. 上課時要坐好,不要_____。（颱風　亂動）

4. 舊金山的氣候好，很少＿＿＿＿＿＿。（颱風　亂動）

八　根據課文判斷對錯

1. 張衡小時候能數幾十顆星星。　　　　　　＿＿對＿＿錯

2. 張衡坐在院子裏，低著頭數星星。　　　　＿＿對＿＿錯

3. 天上的星星是不動的。　　　　　　　　　＿＿對＿＿錯

4. 張衡的地動儀是世界上最早的地震儀器。

　　　　　　　　　　　　　　　　　　　　＿＿對＿＿錯

5. 地動儀用銅製成，上面有四條龍，朝著四個方向。　　　　　　　　　　　　　　　＿＿對＿＿錯

九　朗讀課文三遍

第七課

一 寫生詞

專	家											
寺	院											
敷												
湯												
介	紹											
查	找											
上	吐	下	瀉									

二 組詞

專____　　孤____　　寺____　　劃____

者____　　查____　　吐____　　湯____

介____　　資____　　歷____　　搗____

三 選字組詞

（專　轉）家　　　　　　　　圖（劃　書）

紅（重　腫）　　　　　　　　劃（破　坡）

（搗　島）爛　　　　　　　　（介　界）紹

海（搗　島）　　　　　　　　世（介　界）

（瀉　寫）字　　資（料　斗）　　（孤　狐）兒

四 加上或者變換偏旁，再組詞

例：叮—釘（釘子）

腫—（　　）　湯—（　　）　咬—（　　）

寺—（　　）　畫—（　　）　專—（　　）

五 選擇填空（請把詞語寫在空白處）

1. 陸羽小時候是個_____。（孤兒　狐狸）

2. 小弟弟生病了，上吐下_____的。（瀉　寫）

六 根據課文判斷對錯

1. 唐代有位著名的茶葉專家叫陸羽。　　　＿＿對＿＿錯

2. 陸羽是個孤兒,從小在寺院裏長大。　　＿＿對＿＿錯

3. 陸羽小時候身上有了傷口,用茶葉治,很快就好了。　　＿＿對＿＿錯

4. 茶葉和芥^{jiè}菜花煮的湯可以治病。　　＿＿對＿＿錯

5. 陸羽覺得茶葉很神奇,想寫書介紹茶葉。　　＿＿對＿＿錯

6. 他從古書中找到很多有關茶的資料。　　＿＿對＿＿錯

7. 他又親自到種植茶樹的地區去瞭解茶葉的情況。　　＿＿對＿＿錯

8. 陸羽在家裏,花了四年的時間寫完了《茶經》一書。　　＿＿對＿＿錯

七 造句

1. 不料＿＿＿＿＿＿＿＿＿＿＿＿＿＿＿＿＿＿

2. 互相＿＿＿＿＿＿＿＿＿＿＿＿＿＿＿＿＿＿

八 詞語解釋

不料＿＿＿＿＿＿＿＿＿＿＿＿＿＿＿＿＿＿＿

九　縮寫課文《茶神陸羽》（至少寫八句話）

十　朗讀課文三遍

第九課

一 寫生詞

比	較										
排	尿										
脹											
蔥											
棺	材										
滴											
穴	位										
針	灸										
盲											
缺	少										
維	生	素									
含	有										
記	載										

二 組詞

穴_____　滴_____　含_____　載_____

棺_____　較_____　灸_____　缺_____

素_____　盲_____　敬_____　經_____

三 選字組詞

（匆　蔥）忙　　（棺　官）材　　（脹　張）破

大（匆　蔥）　　（棺　官）員　　一（脹　張）

停（正　止）　　（掃　婦）人　　經（臉　驗）

反（正　止）　　（掃　婦）地　　洗（臉　驗）

四 選擇填空（請把詞語寫在空白處）

1. 別把氣球吹得太大，它會_____的！（破壞　脹破）

2. 水龍頭沒有關好，水一滴一滴往下_____。（滴　沉）

3. 孫思邈成了世界上第一個給病人_____的人。
（piào）

（導尿　開刀）

4. 老年孫思邈將一生行醫的_____寫成了《千金方》一書。　　　　　　　　　　　　　（方法　經驗）

5. 《千金方》一書記載了_____多種藥物和5000多個藥方。　　　　　　　　　　　　　　（800　200）

6. 人們尊敬地稱孫思邈為_____（"藥王"　"茶神"）。

7. 大家越來越_____中文學習。（重視　重量）

8. 曹操想知道大象的_____。（重視　重量）

五　根據課文選擇正確答案（請把答案寫在空白處）

1. _____有位著名的醫學家、藥物學家孫思邈。

　　A 唐代　　　　B 漢朝　　　　C 宋朝

2. 孫思邈用_____導尿，成了世界上第一個給病人導尿的人。

　　A 竹管　　　　B 木棍　　　　C 蔥管

3. 孫思邈給產婦扎針，產婦醒過來了，孩子也生出來了，_____。

　　A 救了婦人　　　B 一針救兩命　　　C 救了孩子

六 根據課文判斷對錯

1. 唐代有位著名的醫學家、藥物學家叫孫思邈。　　＿＿對＿＿錯

2. 孫思邈是世界上首先給病人導尿的人。　　＿＿對＿＿錯

3. 有一次孫思邈一針救了一條人命。　　＿＿對＿＿錯

4. 孫思邈發現米kāng糠和麥fū麩能治好腳氣病。　　＿＿對＿＿錯

5. 孫思邈寫的《千金方》一書中記載了800多種藥物和5000多種藥方。　　＿＿對＿＿錯

6. 人們尊敬地稱孫思邈為"棋王"。　　＿＿對＿＿錯

七 造句

1. 不但……還＿＿＿＿＿＿＿＿＿＿＿＿＿＿＿＿＿＿

2. 重視＿＿＿＿＿＿＿＿＿＿＿＿＿＿＿＿＿＿＿＿

3. 來不及＿＿＿＿＿＿＿＿＿＿＿＿＿＿＿＿＿＿＿

八　縮寫課文《藥王孫思邈》(至少寫十句話,"邈"字可寫漢語拼音)

九　朗讀課文三遍

第十一課

一　寫生詞

都	江	堰									
主	持										
灌	溉										
畝											
岷	江										
災											
窄											
漲											
莊	稼										
壘											
艱	苦										
瓶											

堤										
逼										
沖	垮									
泡										
乖										

二 組詞

持＿＿＿　　利＿＿＿　　瓶＿＿＿　　災＿＿＿

漲＿＿＿　　稼＿＿＿　　艱＿＿＿　　堤＿＿＿

垮＿＿＿　　牢＿＿＿　　灌＿＿＿　　逼＿＿＿

三 選字組詞

回（家　稼）　　水（堤　提）　　（堤　提）包

附（進　近）　　沖（夸　垮）　　（逼　通）著

水（泡　包）　　牢（國　固）　　（乘　乖）法

四 寫出反義詞

寬——　　　　漲——　　　　硬——

五 選擇填空(請把詞語寫在空白處)

1. 公路_____的森林發生了火災。(附近　走進)

2. 我_____新建的體育館,裏面真乾淨。(附近　走進)

3. 河馬_____大嘴時,樣子真嚇人。(張開　上漲)

4. 最近的物價一直在_____。(張開　上漲)
   （漲 jià）

六 根據課文選擇正確答案(請把答案寫在空白處)

1. 都江堰是一個聞名世界的_____。

   A 建築物　　　B 大運河　　　C 水利工程

2. 都江堰在中國_____。

   A 上海　　　　B 四川省　　　C 河北省

3. 都江堰是_____修建的。

   A 2200多年前戰國時代　　　B 唐朝

4. 都江堰是秦國的_____主持修建的。

   A 李時珍　　　B 李春　　　　C 李冰

七 根據課文判斷對錯

1. 都江堰建成以後,岷江還發洪水,當地人生活很苦。　　　___對___錯

2. 李冰不怕辛苦,察看地形、瞭解水情,找到了水災的原因。　　　___對___錯

3. 李冰決定通過開新河道引水到成都平原灌溉田地。　　　___對___錯

4. 李冰帶人把玉壘山挖開了一個大缺口,叫寶瓶口。　　　___對___錯

5. 李冰讓人們編了很多大竹籠,裏邊裝滿鵝卵石,再沉到江裏去。　　　___對___錯

6. 都江堰一直使用到現在,為灌溉成都平原的良田工作著。　　　___對___錯

八 縮寫課文《都江堰》(至少寫十句)

_____

_____

_____

九 朗讀課文三遍

第一課聽寫

第三課聽寫

第五課聽寫

第七課聽寫

第九課聽寫

第十一課聽寫